31 Days of Wisdom & Praise

*Daily readings from the
books of Psalms and Proverbs*

INTERNATIONAL BIBLE SOCIETY
Colorado Springs, Colorado

31 Days of Wisdom and Praise
© 1990 International Bible Society

Photo courtesy of Henderson Publishing,
Colorado Springs, CO © 1990 Henderson Publishing.

Special thanks to:

R. Dean Jones of Spirit-Truth Fellowship
for encouraging the Bible Society
to publish this unique presentation
of Psalms and Proverbs.

Eng. Portion NIV560-
IBS92045000

DAY 1

Psalm 1

1 Blessed is the man
   who does not walk in the counsel of the wicked
or stand in the way of sinners
   or sit in the seat of mockers.
2 But his delight is in the law of the Lord,
   and on his law he meditates day and night.
3 He is like a tree planted by streams of water,
   which yields its fruit in season
and whose leaf does not wither.
   Whatever he does prospers.

4 Not so the wicked!
   They are like chaff
   that the wind blows away.
5 Therefore the wicked will not stand in the
      judgment,
   nor sinners in the assembly of the righteous.

6 For the Lord watches over the way of the righteous,
   but the way of the wicked will perish.

Psalm 31

For the director of music. A psalm of David.

1 In you, O Lord, I have taken refuge;
   let me never be put to shame;
   deliver me in your righteousness.
2 Turn your ear to me,

come quickly to my rescue;
be my rock of refuge,
  a strong fortress to save me.
3 Since you are my rock and my fortress,
  for the sake of your name lead and guide me.
4 Free me from the trap that is set for me,
  for you are my refuge.
5 Into your hands I commit my spirit;
  redeem me, O Lord, the God of truth.
6 I hate those who cling to worthless idols;
  I trust in the Lord.
7 I will be glad and rejoice in your love,
  for you saw my affliction
  and knew the anguish of my soul.
8 You have not handed me over to the enemy
  but have set my feet in a spacious place.

9 Be merciful to me, O Lord, for I am in distress;
  my eyes grow weak with sorrow,
  my soul and my body with grief.
10 My life is consumed by anguish
  and my years by groaning;
  my strength fails because of my affliction, *a*
  and my bones grow weak.
11 Because of all my enemies,
  I am the utter contempt of my neighbors;
  I am a dread to my friends—
  those who see me on the street flee from me.
12 I am forgotten by them as though I were dead;
  I have become like broken pottery.
13 For I hear the slander of many;
  there is terror on every side;

*a*10 Or *guilt*

they conspire against me
and plot to take my life.

14 But I trust in you, O Lord;
I say, "You are my God."
15 My times are in your hands;
deliver me from my enemies
and from those who pursue me.
16 Let your face shine on your servant;
save me in your unfailing love.
17 Let me not be put to shame, O Lord,
for I have cried out to you;
but let the wicked be put to shame
and lie silent in the grave. *a*
18 Let their lying lips be silenced,
for with pride and contempt
they speak arrogantly against the righteous.

19 How great is your goodness,
which you have stored up for those who fear
you,
which you bestow in the sight of men
on those who take refuge in you.
20 In the shelter of your presence you hide them
from the intrigues of men;
in your dwelling you keep them safe
from accusing tongues.

21 Praise be to the Lord,
for he showed his wonderful love to me
when I was in a besieged city.
22 In my alarm I said,
"I am cut off from your sight!"

*a*17 Hebrew *Sheol*

Yet you heard my cry for mercy
  when I called to you for help.

23 Love the Lord, all his saints!
   The Lord preserves the faithful,
     but the proud he pays back in full.
24 Be strong and take heart,
   all you who hope in the Lord.

Psalm 61

For the director of music. With stringed instruments.
Of David.

1 Hear my cry, O God;
   listen to my prayer.

2 From the ends of the earth I call to you,
   I call as my heart grows faint;
     lead me to the rock that is higher than I.

3 For you have been my refuge,
   a strong tower against the foe.

4 I long to dwell in your tent forever
   and take refuge in the shelter of your
     wings.   *Selah*

5 For you have heard my vows, O God;
   you have given me the heritage of those who
     fear your name.

6 Increase the days of the king's life,
   his years for many generations.

7 May he be enthroned in God's presence forever;
   appoint your love and faithfulness to protect him.

8 Then will I ever sing praise to your name
   and fulfill my vows day after day.

Psalm 91

1   He who dwells in the shelter of the Most High
      will rest in the shadow of the Almighty. ^{*a*}

2   I will say ^{*b*} of the Lord, "He is my refuge and my
      fortress,
      my God, in whom I trust."

3   Surely he will save you from the fowler's snare
      and from the deadly pestilence.

4   He will cover you with his feathers,
      and under his wings you will find refuge;
      his faithfulness will be your shield and
      rampart.

5   You will not fear the terror of night,
      nor the arrow that flies by day,

6   nor the pestilence that stalks in the darkness,
      nor the plague that destroys at midday.

7   A thousand may fall at your side,
      ten thousand at your right hand,
      but it will not come near you.

8   You will only observe with your eyes
      and see the punishment of the wicked.

9   If you make the Most High your dwelling—
      even the Lord, who is my refuge—

10   then no harm will befall you,
      no disaster will come near your tent.

11   For he will command his angels concerning you
      to guard you in all your ways;

12   they will lift you up in their hands,
      so that you will not strike your foot against a
      stone.

^{*a*}1 Hebrew *Shaddai*   ^{*b*}2 Or *He says*

13 You will tread upon the lion and the cobra;
    you will trample the great lion and the serpent.

14 "Because he loves me," says the Lord, "I will
       rescue him;
    I will protect him, for he acknowledges my
       name.
15 He will call upon me, and I will answer him;
    I will be with him in trouble,
    I will deliver him and honor him.
16 With long life will I satisfy him
    and show him my salvation."

Psalm 121
A song of ascents.

1 I lift up my eyes to the hills—
    where does my help come from?
2 My help comes from the Lord,
    the Maker of heaven and earth.

3 He will not let your foot slip—
    he who watches over you will not slumber;
4 indeed, he who watches over Israel
    will neither slumber nor sleep.

5 The Lord watches over you—
    the Lord is your shade at your right hand;
6 the sun will not harm you by day,
    nor the moon by night.

7 The Lord will keep you from all harm—
    he will watch over your life;
8 the Lord will watch over your coming
      and going
    both now and forevermore.

Proverbs 1

¹ The proverbs of Solomon son of David, king of Israel:

2   for attaining wisdom and discipline;
      for understanding words of insight;
3   for acquiring a disciplined and prudent life,
      doing what is right and just and fair;
4   for giving prudence to the simple,
      knowledge and discretion to the young—
5   let the wise listen and add to their learning,
      and let the discerning get guidance—
6   for understanding proverbs and parables,
      the sayings and riddles of the wise.

7   The fear of the Lord is the beginning of
        knowledge,
      but fools *a* despise wisdom and discipline.

8   Listen, my son, to your father's instruction
      and do not forsake your mother's teaching.
9   They will be a garland to grace your head
      and a chain to adorn your neck.

10   My son, if sinners entice you,
      do not give in to them.
11   If they say, "Come along with us;
      let's lie in wait for someone's blood,
      let's waylay some harmless soul;
12   let's swallow them alive, like the grave, *b*
      and whole, like those who go down to the pit;

---

*a*7 The Hebrew words rendered *fool* in Proverbs, and often elsewhere in the Old Testament, denote one who is morally deficient.
*b*12 Hebrew *Sheol*

13 we will get all sorts of valuable things
    and fill our houses with plunder;

14 throw in your lot with us,
    and we will share a common purse"—

15 my son, do not go along with them,
    do not set foot on their paths;

16 for their feet rush into sin,
    they are swift to shed blood.

17 How useless to spread a net
    in full view of all the birds!

18 These men lie in wait for their own blood;
    they waylay only themselves!

19 Such is the end of all who go after ill-gotten gain;
    it takes away the lives of those who get it.

20 Wisdom calls aloud in the street,
    she raises her voice in the public squares;

21 at the head of the noisy streets ^a she cries out,
    in the gateways of the city she makes her speech:

22 "How long will you simple ones ^b love your
        simple ways?
    How long will mockers delight in mockery
        and fools hate knowledge?

23 If you had responded to my rebuke,
    I would have poured out my heart to you
        and made my thoughts known to you.

24 But since you rejected me when I called
    and no one gave heed when I stretched out my
        hand,

25 since you ignored all my advice

---

^a21 Hebrew; Septuagint / *on the tops of the walls*   ^b22 The Hebrew
word rendered *simple* in Proverbs generally denotes one without
moral direction and inclined to evil.

and would not accept my rebuke,
26   I in turn will laugh at your disaster;
        I will mock when calamity overtakes you—
27   when calamity overtakes you like a storm,
        when disaster sweeps over you like a
            whirlwind,
        when distress and trouble overwhelm you.

28   "Then they will call to me but I will not answer;
        they will look for me but will not find me.
29   Since they hated knowledge
        and did not choose to fear the Lord,
30   since they would not accept my advice
        and spurned my rebuke,
31   they will eat the fruit of their ways
        and be filled with the fruit of their schemes.
32   For the waywardness of the simple will kill them,
        and the complacency of fools will destroy
            them;
33   but whoever listens to me will live in safety
        and be at ease, without fear of harm."

DAY 2

Psalm 2

1   Why do the nations conspire *a*
        and the peoples plot in vain?
2   The kings of the earth take their stand
        and the rulers gather together
against the Lord
        and against his Anointed One. *b*

a1 Hebrew; Septuagint *rage*   *b2* Or *anointed one*

3 "Let us break their chains," they say,
       "and throw off their fetters."

4 The One enthroned in heaven laughs;
       the Lord scoffs at them.

5 Then he rebukes them in his anger
       and terrifies them in his wrath,
           saying,

6 "I have installed my King *a*
       on Zion, my holy hill."

7 I will proclaim the decree of the Lord:

   He said to me, "You are my Son *b*;
       today I have become your Father. *c*

8 Ask of me,
       and I will make the nations your
           inheritance,
       the ends of the earth your possession.

9 You will rule them with an iron scepter *d*;
       you will dash them to pieces like
           pottery."

10 Therefore, you kings, be wise;
        be warned, you rulers of the earth.

11 Serve the Lord with fear
        and rejoice with trembling.

12 Kiss the Son, lest he be angry
        and you be destroyed in your
            way,
        for his wrath can flare up in a moment.
        Blessed are all who take refuge
            in him.

*a*6 Or *king*   *b*7 Or *son*; also in verse 12   *c*7 Or *have begotten you*
*d*9 Or *will break them with a rod of iron*

Psalm 32
Of David. A *maskil.* [a]

1   Blessed is he
      whose transgressions are forgiven,
      whose sins are covered.
2   Blessed is the man
      whose sin the Lord does not count against him
      and in whose spirit is no deceit.

3   When I kept silent,
      my bones wasted away
      through my groaning all day long.
4   For day and night
      your hand was heavy upon me;
    my strength was sapped
      as in the heat of summer.   *Selah*
5   Then I acknowledged my sin to you
      and did not cover up my iniquity.
    I said, "I will confess
      my transgressions to the Lord"—
    and you forgave
      the guilt of my sin.   *Selah*

6   Therefore let everyone who is godly pray
            to you
      while you may be found;
    surely when the mighty waters rise,
      they will not reach him.
7   You are my hiding place;
      you will protect me from trouble
      and surround me with songs of
            deliverance.   *Selah*

---

[a] Title: Probably a literary or musical term

8   I will instruct you and teach you in the way you
         should go;
      I will counsel you and watch over you.

9   Do not be like the horse or the mule,
      which have no understanding
    but must be controlled by bit and bridle
      or they will not come to you.

10   Many are the woes of the wicked,
      but the Lord's unfailing love surrounds
      the man who trusts in him.

11   Rejoice in the Lord and be glad, you righteous;
      sing, all you who are upright in heart!

Psalm 62

For the director of music. For Jeduthun.
A psalm of David.

1   My soul finds rest in God alone;
      my salvation comes from him.

2   He alone is my rock and my salvation;
      he is my fortress, I will never be shaken.

3   How long will you assault a man?
      Would all of you throw him down—
      this leaning wall, this tottering fence?

4   They fully intend to topple him
      from his lofty place;
      they take delight in lies.
    With their mouths they bless,
      but in their hearts they curse.   *Selah*

5   Find rest, O my soul, in God alone;
      My hope comes from him.

6   He alone is my rock and my salvation;

he is my fortress, I will not be shaken.

7   My salvation and my honor depend on God [a];
       he is my mighty rock, my refuge.

8   Trust in him at all times, O people;
       pour out your hearts to him,
           for God is our refuge.   *Selah*

9   Lowborn men are but a breath,
       the highborn are but a lie;
    if weighed on a balance, they are nothing;
       together they are only a breath.

10 Do not trust in extortion
       or take pride in stolen goods;
    though your riches increase,
       do not set your heart on them.

11 One thing God has spoken,
       two things have I heard:
    that you, O God, are strong,

12 and that you, O Lord, are loving.
    Surely you will reward each person
       according to what he has done.

Psalm 92

A psalm. A song. For the Sabbath day.

1   It is good to praise the Lord
       and make music to your name,
           O Most High,

2   to proclaim your love in the morning
       and your faithfulness at night,

3   to the music of the ten-stringed lyre
       and the melody of the harp.

[a]7 Or / *God Most High is my salvation and my honor*

4   For you make me glad by your deeds,
        O Lord;
      I sing for joy at the works of your hands.
5   How great are your works, O Lord,
        how profound your thoughts!
6   The senseless man does not know,
        fools do not understand,
7   that though the wicked spring up like grass
        and all evildoers flourish,
      they will be forever destroyed.

8   But you, O Lord, are exalted forever.

9   For surely your enemies, O Lord,
        surely your enemies will perish;
      all evildoers will be scattered.
10 You have exalted my horn *a* like that of a
        wild ox;
      fine oils have been poured upon me.
11 My eyes have seen the defeat of my
        adversaries;
      my ears have heard the rout of my
        wicked foes.

12 The righteous will flourish like a palm tree,
        they will grow like a cedar of Lebanon;
13 planted in the house of the Lord,
        they will flourish in the courts of our God.
14 They will still bear fruit in old age,
        they will stay fresh and green,
15 proclaiming, "The Lord is upright;
        he is my Rock, and there is no wickedness
        in him."

a10 Horn here symbolizes strength.

Psalm 122
A song of ascents. Of David.

1 I rejoiced with those who said to me,
      "Let us go to the house of the Lord."
2 Our feet are standing
      in your gates, O Jerusalem.

3 Jerusalem is built like a city
      that is closely compacted together.
4 That is where the tribes go up,
      the tribes of the Lord,
   to praise the name of the Lord
      according to the statute given to Israel.
5 There the thrones for judgment stand,
      the thrones of the house of David.

6 Pray for the peace of Jerusalem:
      "May those who love you be secure.
7 May there be peace within your walls
      and security within your citadels."
8 For the sake of my brothers and friends,
      I will say, "Peace be within you."
9 For the sake of the house of the Lord our God,
      I will seek your prosperity.

Proverbs 2

1 My son, if you accept my words
      and store up my commands within you,
2 turning your ear to wisdom
      and applying your heart to understanding,
3 and if you call out for insight
      and cry aloud for understanding,
4 and if you look for it as for silver

and search for it as for hidden treasure,
5 then you will understand the fear of the Lord
and find the knowledge of God.
6 For the Lord gives wisdom,
and from his mouth come knowledge and
understanding.
7 He holds victory in store for the upright,
he is a shield to those whose walk is blameless,
8 for he guards the course of the just
and protects the way of his faithful ones.

9 Then you will understand what is right and just
and fair—every good path.
10 For wisdom will enter your heart,
and knowledge will be pleasant to your soul.
11 Discretion will protect you,
and understanding will guard you.

12 Wisdom will save you from the ways of wicked men,
from men whose words are perverse,
13 who leave the straight paths
to walk in dark ways,
14 who delight in doing wrong
and rejoice in the perverseness of evil,
15 whose paths are crooked
and who are devious in their ways.

16 It will save you also from the adulteress,
from the wayward wife with her seductive
words,
17 who has left the partner of her youth
and ignored the covenant she made before
God. *a*

*a*17 Or *covenant of her God*

18 For her house leads down to death
   and her paths to the spirits of the dead.
19 None who go to her return
   or attain the paths of life.

20 Thus you will walk in the ways of good men
   and keep to the paths of the righteous.
21 For the upright will live in the land,
   and the blameless will remain in it;
22 but the wicked will be cut off from the land,
   and the unfaithful will be torn from it.

DAY 3

Psalm 3
A psalm of David. When he fled from his son
Absalom.

1   O Lord, how many are my foes!
   How many rise up against me!
2   Many are saying of me,
   "God will not deliver him."   *Selah* [a]

3   But you are a shield around me, O Lord;
   you bestow glory on me and lift [b] up
   my head.
4   To the Lord I cry aloud,
   and he answers me from his holy hill.   *Selah*

5   I lie down and sleep;
   I wake again, because the Lord sustains me.

---

[a]2 A word of uncertain meaning, occurring frequently in the Psalms;
possibly a musical term   [b]3 Or *Lord, / my Glorious One, who lifts*

6   I will not fear the tens of thousands
        drawn up against me on every side.

7   Arise, O Lord!
        Deliver me, O my God!
    Strike all my enemies on the jaw;
        break the teeth of the wicked.

8   From the Lord comes deliverance.
        May your blessing be on your people.   *Selah*

Psalm 33

1   Sing joyfully to the Lord, you righteous;
        it is fitting for the upright to praise him.
2   Praise the Lord with the harp;
        make music to him on the ten-stringed lyre.
3   Sing to him a new song;
        play skillfully, and shout for joy.

4   For the word of the Lord is right and true;
        he is faithful in all he does.
5   The Lord loves righteousness and justice;
        the earth is full of his unfailing love.

6   By the word of the Lord were the heavens made,
        their starry host by the breath of his mouth.
7   He gathers the waters of the sea into jars [a];
        he puts the deep into storehouses.
8   Let all the earth fear the Lord;
        let all the people of the world revere him.
9   For he spoke, and it came to be;
        he commanded, and it stood firm.
10 The Lord foils the plans of the nations;

[a]7 Or *sea as into a heap*

he thwarts the purposes of the peoples.
11 But the plans of the Lord stand firm forever,
the purposes of his heart through all generations.

12 Blessed is the nation whose God is the Lord,
the people he chose for his inheritance.
13 From heaven the Lord looks down
and sees all mankind;
14 from his dwelling place he watches
all who live on earth—
15 he who forms the hearts of all,
who considers everything they do.
16 No king is saved by the size of his army;
no warrior escapes by his great strength.
17 A horse is a vain hope for deliverance;
despite all its great strength it cannot save.
18 But the eyes of the Lord are on those who fear him,
on those whose hope is in his unfailing love,
19 to deliver them from death
and keep them alive in famine.

20 We wait in hope for the Lord;
he is our help and our shield.
21 In him our hearts rejoice,
for we trust in his holy name.
22 May your unfailing love rest upon us, O Lord,
even as we put our hope in you.

Psalm 63
A psalm of David. When he was
in the Desert of Judah.

1 O God, you are my God,
earnestly I seek you;
my soul thirsts for you,

    my body longs for you,
in a dry and weary land
    where there is no water.

2 I have seen you in the sanctuary
    and beheld your power and your glory.
3 Because your love is better than life,
    my lips will glorify you.
4 I will praise you as long as I live,
    and in your name I will lift up my hands.
5 My soul will be satisfied as with the richest of
      foods;
    with singing lips my mouth will praise you.
6 On my bed I remember you;
    I think of you through the watches of the night.
7 Because you are my help,
    I sing in the shadow of your wings.

8 My soul clings to you;
    your right hand upholds me.
9 They who seek my life will be destroyed;
    they will go down to the depths of the earth.
10 They will be given over to the sword
    and become food for jackals.

11 But the king will rejoice in God;
    all who swear by God's name will praise him,
    while the mouths of liars will be silenced.

Psalm 93

1 The Lord reigns, he is robed in majesty;
    the Lord is robed in majesty
    and is armed with strength.
The world is firmly established;

  it cannot be moved.
2 Your throne was established long ago;
     you are from all eternity.

3 The seas have lifted up, O Lord,
     the seas have lifted up their voice;
     the seas have lifted up their pounding waves.
4 Mightier than the thunder of the great waters,
     mightier than the breakers of the sea—
     the Lord on high is mighty.

5 Your statutes stand firm;
     holiness adorns your house
     for endless days, O Lord.

Psalm 123
A song of ascents.

1 I lift up my eyes to you,
     to you whose throne is in heaven.
2 As the eyes of slaves look to the hand of their master,
     as the eyes of a maid look to the hand of her
       mistress,
   so our eyes look to the Lord our God,
     till he shows us his mercy.

3 Have mercy on us, O Lord, have mercy on us,
     for we have endured much contempt.
4 We have endured much ridicule from the proud,
     much contempt from the arrogant.

Proverbs 3

1 My son, do not forget my teaching,
     but keep my commands in your heart,

2   for they will prolong your life many years
        and bring you prosperity.

3   Let love and faithfulness never leave you;
        bind them around your neck,
        write them on the tablet of your heart.

4   Then you will win favor and a good name
        in the sight of God and man.

5   Trust in the Lord with all your heart
        and lean not on your own understanding;

6   in all your ways acknowledge him,
        and he will make your paths straight. [a]

7   Do not be wise in your own eyes;
        fear the Lord and shun evil.

8   This will bring health to your body
        and nourishment to your bones.

9   Honor the Lord with your wealth,
        with the firstfruits of all your crops;

10   then your barns will be filled to overflowing,
        and your vats will brim over with new wine.

11   My son, do not despise the Lord's discipline
        and do not resent his rebuke,

12   because the Lord disciplines those he loves,
        as a father [b] the son he delights in.

13   Blessed is the man who finds wisdom,
        the man who gains understanding,

14   for she is more profitable than silver
        and yields better returns than gold.

15   She is more precious than rubies;

---

[a]6 Or *will direct your paths*   [b]12 Hebrew; Septuagint / *and he punishes*

nothing you desire can compare with her.

16 Long life is in her right hand;
    in her left hand are riches and honor.

17 Her ways are pleasant ways,
    and all her paths are peace.

18 She is a tree of life to those who embrace her;
    those who lay hold of her will be blessed.

19 By wisdom the Lord laid the earth's foundations,
    by understanding he set the heavens in place;

20 by his knowledge the deeps were divided,
    and the clouds let drop the dew.

21 My son, preserve sound judgment and discernment,
    do not let them out of your sight;

22 they will be life for you,
    an ornament to grace your neck.

23 Then you will go on your way in safety,
    and your foot will not stumble;

24 when you lie down, you will not be afraid;
    when you lie down, your sleep will be sweet.

25 Have no fear of sudden disaster
    or of the ruin that overtakes the wicked,

26 for the Lord will be your confidence
    and will keep your foot from being snared.

27 Do not withhold good from those who deserve it,
    when it is in your power to act.

28 Do not say to your neighbor,
    "Come back later; I'll give it tomorrow"—
    when you now have it with you.

29 Do not plot harm against your neighbor,
    who lives trustfully near you.

30 Do not accuse a man for no reason—
    when he has done you no harm.

31 Do not envy a violent man
   or choose any of his ways,
32 for the Lord detests a perverse man
   but takes the upright into his confidence.

33 The Lord's curse is on the house of the wicked,
   but he blesses the home of the righteous.
34 He mocks proud mockers
   but gives grace to the humble.
35 The wise inherit honor,
   but fools he holds up to shame.

DAY 4

Psalm 4
For the director of music. With stringed instruments.
A psalm of David.

1 Answer me when I call to you,
   O my righteous God.
   Give me relief from my distress;
   be merciful to me and hear my prayer.

2 How long, O men, will you turn my glory into
   shame ^{a}?
   How long will you love delusions
   and seek false gods ^{b}?   *Selah*

3 Know that the Lord has set apart the godly for
   himself;
   the Lord will hear when I call to him.

4 In your anger do not sin;
   when you are on your beds,

^{a}2 Or *you dishonor my Glorious One* ^{b}2 Or *seek lies*

search your hearts and be silent. *Selah*

5 Offer right sacrifices
and trust in the Lord.

6 Many are asking, "Who can show us any good?"
Let the light of your face shine upon us, O Lord.

7 You have filled my heart with greater joy
than when their grain and new wine abound.

8 I will lie down and sleep in peace,
for you alone, O Lord,
make me dwell in safety.

Psalm 34 [a]

Of David. When he pretended to be insane before
Abimelech, who drove him away, and he left.

1 I will extol the Lord at all times;
his praise will always be on my lips.

2 My soul will boast in the Lord;
let the afflicted hear and rejoice.

3 Glorify the Lord with me;
let us exalt his name together.

4 I sought the Lord, and he answered me;
he delivered me from all my fears.

5 Those who look to him are radiant;
their faces are never covered with shame.

6 This poor man called, and the Lord heard him;
he saved him out of all his troubles.

7 The angel of the Lord encamps around those who
fear him,
and he delivers them.

[a] This psalm is an acrostic poem, the verses of which begin with the
successive letters of the Hebrew alphabet.

8 Taste and see that the Lord is good;
      blessed is the man who takes refuge in him.
9 Fear the Lord, you his saints,
      for those who fear him lack nothing.
10 The lions may grow weak and hungry,
      but those who seek the Lord lack no good thing.

11 Come, my children, listen to me;
      I will teach you the fear of the Lord.
12 Whoever of you loves life
      and desires to see many good days,
13 keep your tongue from evil
      and your lips from speaking lies.
14 Turn from evil and do good;
      seek peace and pursue it.

15 The eyes of the Lord are on the righteous
      and his ears are attentive to their cry;
16 the face of the Lord is against those who do evil,
      to cut off the memory of them from the earth.

17 The righteous cry out, and the Lord hears them;
      he delivers them from all their troubles.
18 The Lord is close to the brokenhearted
      and saves those who are crushed in spirit.

19 A righteous man may have many troubles,
      but the Lord delivers him from them all;
20 he protects all his bones,
      not one of them will be broken.

21 Evil will slay the wicked;
      the foes of the righteous will be condemned.
22 The Lord redeems his servants;
      no one will be condemned who takes refuge in
         him.

Psalm 64

For the director of music. A psalm of David.

1 Hear me, O God, as I voice my complaint;
     protect my life from the threat of the enemy.

2 Hide me from the conspiracy of the wicked,
     from that noisy crowd of evildoers.

3 They sharpen their tongues like swords
     and aim their words like deadly arrows.

4 They shoot from ambush at the innocent man;
     they shoot at him suddenly, without fear.

5 They encourage each other in evil plans,
     they talk about hiding their snares;
     they say, "Who will see them [a]?"

6 They plot injustice and say,
     "We have devised a perfect plan!"
     Surely the mind and heart of man are
       cunning.

7 But God will shoot them with arrows;
     suddenly they will be struck down.

8 He will turn their own tongues against them
     and bring them to ruin;
     all who see them will shake their heads
       in scorn.

9 All mankind will fear;
     they will proclaim the works of God
     and ponder what he has done.

10 Let the righteous rejoice in the Lord
     and take refuge in him;
     let all the upright in heart praise him!

[a]5 Or *us*

Psalm 94

1   O Lord, the God who avenges,
     O God who avenges, shine forth.
2   Rise up, O Judge of the earth;
     pay back to the proud what they deserve.
3   How long will the wicked, O Lord,
     how long will the wicked be jubilant?

4   They pour out arrogant words;
     all the evildoers are full of boasting.
5   They crush your people, O Lord;
     they oppress your inheritance.
6   They slay the widow and the alien;
     they murder the fatherless.
7   They say, "The Lord does not see;
     the God of Jacob pays no heed."

8   Take heed, you senseless ones among the people;
     you fools, when will you become wise?
9   Does he who implanted the ear not hear?
     Does he who formed the eye not see?
10   Does he who disciplines nations not punish?
     Does he who teaches man lack knowledge?
11   The Lord knows the thoughts of man;
     he knows that they are futile.

12   Blessed is the man you discipline, O Lord,
     the man you teach from your law;
13   you grant him relief from days of trouble,
     till a pit is dug for the wicked.
14   For the Lord will not reject his people;
     he will never forsake his inheritance.
15   Judgment will again be founded on
      righteousness,
     and all the upright in heart will follow it.

16 Who will rise up for me against the wicked?
   Who will take a stand for me against evildoers?
17 Unless the Lord had given me help,
   I would soon have dwelt in the silence of death.
18 When I said, "My foot is slipping,"
   your love, O Lord, supported me.
19 When anxiety was great within me,
   your consolation brought joy to my soul.

20 Can a corrupt throne be allied with you—
   one that brings on misery by its decrees?
21 They band together against the righteous
   and condemn the innocent to death.
22 But the Lord has become my fortress,
   and my God the rock in whom I take refuge.
23 He will repay them for their sins
   and destroy them for their wickedness;
   the Lord our God will destroy them.

Psalm 124

A song of ascents. Of David.

1 If the Lord had not been on our side—
   let Israel say—
2 if the Lord had not been on our side
   when men attacked us,
3 when their anger flared against us,
   they would have swallowed us alive;
4 the flood would have engulfed us,
   the torrent would have swept over us,
5 the raging waters would have swept us away.

6 Praise be to the Lord,
   who has not let us be torn by their teeth.
7 We have escaped like a bird

out of the fowler's snare;
the snare has been broken,
and we have escaped.
8 Our help is in the name of the Lord,
the Maker of heaven and earth.

Proverbs 4

1 Listen, my sons, to a father's instruction;
pay attention and gain understanding.
2 I give you sound learning,
so do not forsake my teaching.
3 When I was a boy in my father's house,
still tender, and an only child of my mother,
4 he taught me and said,
"Lay hold of my words with all your heart;
keep my commands and you will live.
5 Get wisdom, get understanding;
do not forget my words or swerve from them.
6 Do not forsake wisdom, and she will protect you;
love her, and she will watch over you.
7 Wisdom is supreme; therefore get wisdom.
Though it cost all you have, [a] get understanding.
8 Esteem her, and she will exalt you;
embrace her, and she will honor you.
9 She will set a garland of grace on your head
and present you with a crown of splendor."

10 Listen, my son, accept what I say,
and the years of your life will be many.
11 I guide you in the way of wisdom
and lead you along straight paths.

---

[a]7 Or *Whatever else you get*

12 When you walk, your steps will not be hampered;
      when you run, you will not stumble.
13 Hold on to instruction, do not let it go;
      guard it well, for it is your life.
14 Do not set foot on the path of the wicked
      or walk in the way of evil men.
15 Avoid it, do not travel on it;
      turn from it and go on your way.
16 For they cannot sleep till they do evil;
      they are robbed of slumber till they make
         someone fall.
17 They eat the bread of wickedness
      and drink the wine of violence.

18 The path of the righteous is like the first gleam of
         dawn,
      shining ever brighter till the full light of day.
19 But the way of the wicked is like deep darkness;
      they do not know what makes them stumble.

20 My son, pay attention to what I say;
      listen closely to my words.
21 Do not let them out of your sight,
      keep them within your heart;
22 for they are life to those who find them
      and health to a man's whole body.
23 Above all else, guard your heart,
      for it is the wellspring of life.
24 Put away perversity from your mouth;
      keep corrupt talk far from your lips.
25 Let your eyes look straight ahead,
      fix your gaze directly before you.
26 Make level *a* paths for your feet

a26 Or *Consider the*

and take only ways that are firm.
27 Do not swerve to the right or the left;
keep your foot from evil.

DAY 5

Psalm 5

For the director of music. For flutes.
A psalm of David.

1 Give ear to my words, O Lord,
consider my sighing.
2 Listen to my cry for help,
my King and my God,
for to you I pray.
3 In the morning, O Lord, you hear my voice;
in the morning I lay my requests before you
and wait in expectation.

4 You are not a God who takes pleasure in evil;
with you the wicked cannot dwell.
5 The arrogant cannot stand in your presence;
you hate all who do wrong.
6 You destroy those who tell lies;
bloodthirsty and deceitful men
the Lord abhors.

7 But I, by your great mercy,
will come into your house;
in reverence will I bow down
toward your holy temple.
8 Lead me, O Lord, in your righteousness
because of my enemies—
make straight your way before me.

9   Not a word from their mouth can be trusted;
        their heart is filled with destruction.
    Their throat is an open grave;
        with their tongue they speak deceit.
10 Declare them guilty, O God!
        Let their intrigues be their downfall.
    Banish them for their many sins,
        for they have rebelled against you.

11 But let all who take refuge in you be glad;
        let them ever sing for joy.
    Spread your protection over them,
        that those who love your name may rejoice in you.
12 For surely, O Lord, you bless the righteous;
        you surround them with your favor as with a
            shield.

Psalm 35
Of David.

1   Contend, O Lord, with those who contend with me;
        fight against those who fight against me.
2   Take up shield and buckler;
        arise and come to my aid.
3   Brandish spear and javelin *a*
        against those who pursue me.
    Say to my soul,
        "I am your salvation."

4   May those who seek my life
        be disgraced and put to shame;
    may those who plot my ruin
        be turned back in dismay.

a3 Or and block the way

5 May they be like chaff before the wind,
      with the angel of the Lord driving them away;
6 may their path be dark and slippery,
      with the angel of the Lord pursuing them.
7 Since they hid their net for me without cause
      and without cause dug a pit for me,
8 may ruin overtake them by surprise—
      may the net they hid entangle them,
      may they fall into the pit, to their ruin.
9 Then my soul will rejoice in the Lord
      and delight in his salvation.
10 My whole being will exclaim,
      "Who is like you, O Lord?
      You rescue the poor from those too strong for them,
      the poor and needy from those who rob them."

11 Ruthless witnesses come forward;
      they question me on things I know nothing about.
12 They repay me evil for good
      and leave my soul forlorn.
13 Yet when they were ill, I put on sackcloth
      and humbled myself with fasting.
      When my prayers returned to me unanswered,
14   I went about mourning
      as though for my friend or brother.
      I bowed my head in grief
      as though weeping for my mother.
15 But when I stumbled, they gathered in glee;
      attackers gathered against me when I was
         unaware.
      They slandered me without ceasing.
16 Like the ungodly they maliciously mocked *a*;

a16 Septuagint; Hebrew may mean *ungodly circle of mockers.*

they gnashed their teeth at me.
17 O Lord, how long will you look on?
    Rescue my life from their ravages,
        my precious life from these lions.
18 I will give you thanks in the great assembly;
    among throngs of people I will praise you.

19 Let not those gloat over me
        who are my enemies without cause;
    let not those who hate me without reason
        maliciously wink the eye.
20 They do not speak peaceably,
        but devise false accusations
    against those who live quietly in the land.
21 They gape at me and say, "Aha! Aha!
        With our own eyes we have seen it."

22 O Lord, you have seen this; be not silent.
        Do not be far from me, O Lord.
23 Awake, and rise to my defense!
        Contend for me, my God and Lord.
24 Vindicate me in your righteousness, O Lord my
        God;
    do not let them gloat over me.
25 Do not let them think, "Aha, just what we wanted!"
        or say, "We have swallowed him up."

26 May all who gloat over my distress
        be put to shame and confusion;
    may all who exalt themselves over me
        be clothed with shame and disgrace.
27 May those who delight in my vindication
        shout for joy and gladness;
    may they always say, "The Lord be exalted,
        who delights in the well-being of his servant."

28 My tongue will speak of your righteousness
and of your praises all day long.

Psalm 65

For the director of music. A psalm of David. A song.

1 Praise awaits *a* you, O God, in Zion;
to you our vows will be fulfilled.

2 O you who hear prayer,
to you all men will come.

3 When we were overwhelmed by sins,
you forgave *b* our transgressions.

4 Blessed are those you choose
and bring near to live in your courts!
We are filled with the good things of
your house,
of your holy temple.

5 You answer us with awesome deeds of
righteousness,
O God our Savior,
the hope of all the ends of the earth
and of the farthest seas,

6 who formed the mountains by your power,
having armed yourself with strength,

7 who stilled the roaring of the seas,
the roaring of their waves,
and the turmoil of the nations.

8 Those living far away fear your wonders;
where morning dawns and evening fades
you call forth songs of joy.

*a*1 Or *befits*; the meaning of the Hebrew for this word is uncertain.
*b*3 Or *made atonement for*

9   You care for the land and water it;
     you enrich it abundantly.
  The streams of God are filled with water
     to provide the people with grain,
     for so you have ordained it. [a]

10 You drench its furrows
     and level its ridges;
  you soften it with showers
     and bless its crops.

11 You crown the year with your bounty,
     and your carts overflow with abundance.

12 The grasslands of the desert overflow;
     the hills are clothed with gladness.

13 The meadows are covered with flocks
     and the valleys are mantled with grain;
     they shout for joy and sing.

Psalm 95

1   Come, let us sing for joy to the Lord;
     let us shout aloud to the Rock of our salvation.

2   Let us come before him with thanksgiving
     and extol him with music and song.

3   For the Lord is the great God,
     the great King above all gods.

4   In his hand are the depths of the earth,
     and the mountain peaks belong to him.

5   The sea is his, for he made it,
     and his hands formed the dry land.

6   Come, let us bow down in worship,
     let us kneel before the Lord our Maker;

[a]9 Or *for that is how you prepare the land*

7   for he is our God
        and we are the people of his pasture,
        the flock under his care.

    Today, if you hear his voice,
8   do not harden your hearts as you did at
            Meribah, *a*
        as you did that day at Massah *b* in the desert,
9   where your fathers tested and tried me,
        though they had seen what I did.
10   For forty years I was angry with that generation;
        I said, "They are a people whose hearts go
            astray,
        and they have not known my ways."
11   So I declared on oath in my anger,
        "They shall never enter my rest."

Psalm 125
A song of ascents.

1   Those who trust in the Lord are like Mount Zion,
        which cannot be shaken but endures forever.

2   As the mountains surround Jerusalem,
        so the Lord surrounds his people
        both now and forevermore.

3   The scepter of the wicked will not remain
        over the land allotted to the righteous,
    for then the righteous might use
        their hands to do evil.

4   Do good, O Lord, to those who are good,
        to those who are upright in heart.

---

a8 Meribah means *quarreling.*   *a8 Massah* means *testing.*

5   But those who turn to crooked ways
        the Lord will banish with the evildoers.

    Peace be upon Israel.

Proverbs 5

1   My son, pay attention to my wisdom,
        listen well to my words of insight,
2   that you may maintain discretion
        and your lips may preserve knowledge.
3   For the lips of an adulteress drip honey,
        and her speech is smoother than oil;
4   but in the end she is bitter as gall,
        sharp as a double-edged sword.
5   Her feet go down to death;
        her steps lead straight to the grave. *a*
6   She gives no thought to the way of life;
        her paths are crooked, but she knows it not.

7   Now then, my sons, listen to me;
        do not turn aside from what I say.
8   Keep to a path far from her,
        do not go near the door of her house,
9   lest you give your best strength to others
        and your years to one who is cruel,
10 lest strangers feast on your wealth
        and your toil enrich another man's house.
11 At the end of your life you will groan,
        when your flesh and body are spent.
12 You will say, "How I hated discipline!
        How my heart spurned correction!
13 I would not obey my teachers

a5 Hebrew *Sheol*

or listen to my instructors.
14 I have come to the brink of utter ruin
in the midst of the whole assembly."

15 Drink water from your own cistern,
running water from your own well.
16 Should your springs overflow in the streets,
your streams of water in the public squares?
17 Let them be yours alone,
never to be shared with strangers.
18 May your fountain be blessed,
and may you rejoice in the wife of your youth.
19 A loving doe, a graceful deer—
may her breasts satisfy you always,
may you ever be captivated by her love.
20 Why be captivated, my son, by an adulteress?
Why embrace the bosom of another man's
wife?

21 For a man's ways are in full view of the Lord,
and he examines all his paths.
22 The evil deeds of a wicked man ensnare him;
the cords of his sin hold him fast.
23 He will die for lack of discipline,
led astray by his own great folly.

DAY 6

Psalm 6

For the director of music. With stringed instruments.
According to *sheminith*. [a] A psalm of David.

1   O Lord, do not rebuke me in your anger
     or discipline me in your wrath.
2   Be merciful to me, Lord, for I am faint;
     O Lord, heal me, for my bones are in agony.
3   My soul is in anguish.
     How long, O Lord, how long?

4   Turn, O Lord, and deliver me;
     save me because of your unfailing love.
5   No one remembers you when he is dead.
     Who praises you from the grave [b]?

6   I am worn out from groaning;
     all night long I flood my bed with weeping
     and drench my couch with tears.
7   My eyes grow weak with sorrow;
     they fail because of all my foes.

8   Away from me, all you who do evil,
     for the Lord has heard my weeping.
9   The Lord has heard my cry for mercy;
     the Lord accepts my prayer.
10   All my enemies will be ashamed and dismayed;
     they will turn back in sudden disgrace.

[a] Title: Probably a musical term   [b] 5 Hebrew *Sheol*

Psalm 36

For the director of music. Of David
the servant of the Lord.

1 An oracle is within my heart
      concerning the sinfulness of the wicked: [a]
   There is no fear of God
      before his eyes.

2 For in his own eyes he flatters himself
      too much to detect or hate his sin.

3 The words of his mouth are wicked and deceitful;
      he has ceased to be wise and to do good.

4 Even on his bed he plots evil;
      he commits himself to a sinful course
      and does not reject what is wrong.

5 Your love, O Lord, reaches to the heavens,
      your faithfulness to the skies.

6 Your righteousness is like the mighty mountains,
      your justice like the great deep.
   O Lord, you preserve both man and beast.

7   How priceless is your unfailing love!
   Both high and low among men
      find [b] refuge in the shadow of your wings.

8 They feast on the abundance of your house;
      you give them drink from your river of delights.

9 For with you is the fountain of life;
      in your light we see light.

10 Continue your love to those who know you,
      your righteousness to the upright in heart.

11 May the foot of the proud not come against me,

---

[a]1 Or *heart: / Sin proceeds from the wicked.*   [b]7 Or *love, O God! / Men
find; or love! / Both heavenly beings and men / find*

> nor the hand of the wicked drive me away.
12 See how the evildoers lie fallen—
> thrown down, not able to rise!

Psalm 66

For the director of music. A song. A psalm.

1 Shout with joy to God, all the earth!
2   Sing the glory of his name;
> make his praise glorious!
3 Say to God, "How awesome are your deeds!
> So great is your power
> that your enemies cringe before you.
4 All the earth bows down to you;
> they sing praise to you,
> they sing praise to your name."   *Selah*

5 Come and see what God has done,
> how awesome his works in man's behalf!
6 He turned the sea into dry land,
> they passed through the waters on foot—
> come, let us rejoice in him.
7 He rules forever by his power,
> his eyes watch the nations—
> let not the rebellious rise up against him.   *Selah*

8 Praise our God, O peoples,
> let the sound of his praise be heard;
9 he has preserved our lives
> and kept our feet from slipping.
10 For you, O God, tested us;
> you refined us like silver.
11 You brought us into prison
> and laid burdens on our backs.
12 You let men ride over our heads;

we went through fire and water,
but you brought us to a place of abundance.

13 I will come to your temple with burnt offerings
and fulfill my vows to you—
14 vows my lips promised and my mouth spoke
when I was in trouble.
15 I will sacrifice fat animals to you
and an offering of rams;
I will offer bulls and goats.   *Selah*

16 Come and listen, all you who fear God;
let me tell you what he has done for me.
17 I cried out to him with my mouth;
his praise was on my tongue.
18 If I had cherished sin in my heart,
the Lord would not have listened;
19 but God has surely listened
and heard my voice in prayer.
20 Praise be to God,
who has not rejected my prayer
or withheld his love from me!

Psalm 96

1 Sing to the Lord a new song;
sing to the Lord, all the earth.
2 Sing to the Lord, praise his name;
proclaim his salvation day after day.
3 Declare his glory among the nations,
his marvelous deeds among all peoples.

4 For great is the Lord and most worthy of praise;
he is to be feared above all gods.
5 For all the gods of the nations are idols,

but the Lord made the heavens.
6   Splendor and majesty are before him;
strength and glory are in his sanctuary.

7   Ascribe to the Lord, O families of nations,
ascribe to the Lord glory and strength.
8   Ascribe to the Lord the glory due his name;
bring an offering and come into his courts.
9   Worship the Lord in the splendor of his *a* holiness;
tremble before him, all the earth.

10   Say among the nations, "The Lord reigns."
The world is firmly established, it cannot be
moved;
he will judge the peoples with equity.
11   Let the heavens rejoice, let the earth be glad;
let the sea resound, and all that is in it;
12   let the fields be jubilant, and everything in them.
Then all the trees of the forest will sing for joy;
13   they will sing before the Lord, for he comes,
he comes to judge the earth.
He will judge the world in righteousness
and the peoples in his truth.

Psalm 126
A song of ascents.

1   When the Lord brought back the captives to *b*
Zion,
we were like men who dreamed. *c*
2   Our mouths were filled with laughter,
our tongues with songs of joy.

---

a9 Or *Lord with the splendor of*   *b1* Or *Lord restored the fortunes of*
c1 Or *men restored to health*

Then it was said among the nations,
"The Lord has done great things for them."
3 The Lord has done great things for us,
and we are filled with joy.

4 Restore our fortunes, [a] O Lord,
like streams in the Negev.
5 Those who sow in tears
will reap with songs of joy.
6 He who goes out weeping,
carrying seed to sow,
will return with songs of joy,
carrying sheaves with him.

Proverbs 6

1 My son, if you have put up security for your
neighbor,
if you have struck hands in pledge for another,
2 if you have been trapped by what you said,
ensnared by the words of your mouth,
3 then do this, my son, to free yourself,
since you have fallen into your neighbor's hands:
Go and humble yourself;
press your plea with your neighbor!
4 Allow no sleep to your eyes,
no slumber to your eyelids.
5 Free yourself, like a gazelle from the hand of the
hunter,
like a bird from the snare of the fowler.

6 Go to the ant, you sluggard;
consider its ways and be wise!

[a]4 Or Bring back our captives

7   It has no commander,
      no overseer or ruler,

8   yet it stores its provisions in summer
      and gathers its food at harvest.

9   How long will you lie there, you sluggard?
      When will you get up from your sleep?

10 A little sleep, a little slumber,
      a little folding of the hands to rest—

11 and poverty will come on you like a bandit
      and scarcity like an armed man. *a*

12 A scoundrel and villain,
      who goes about with a corrupt mouth,

13 who winks with his eye,
      signals with his feet
      and motions with his fingers,

14 who plots evil with deceit in his heart—
      he always stirs up dissension.

15 Therefore disaster will overtake him in an instant;
      he will suddenly be destroyed—without
         remedy.

16 There are six things the Lord hates,
      seven that are detestable to him:

17   haughty eyes,
         a lying tongue,
         hands that shed innocent blood,

18   a heart that devises wicked schemes,
         feet that are quick to rush into evil,

19   a false witness who pours out lies
         and a man who stirs up dissension among
            brothers.

---

*a*11 Or *like a vagrant / and scarcity like a beggar*

20 My son, keep your father's commands
    and do not forsake your mother's teaching.
21 Bind them upon your heart forever;
    fasten them around your neck.
22 When you walk, they will guide you;
    when you sleep, they will watch over you;
    when you awake, they will speak to you.
23 For these commands are a lamp,
    this teaching is a light,
and the corrections of discipline
    are the way to life,
24 keeping you from the immoral woman,
    from the smooth tongue of the wayward wife.
25 Do not lust in your heart after her beauty
    or let her captivate you with her eyes,
26 for the prostitute reduces you to a loaf of bread,
    and the adulteress preys upon your very life.
27 Can a man scoop fire into his lap
    without his clothes being burned?
28 Can a man walk on hot coals
    without his feet being scorched?
29 So is he who sleeps with another man's wife;
    no one who touches her will go unpunished.

30 Men do not despise a thief if he steals
    to satisfy his hunger when he is starving.
31 Yet if he is caught, he must pay sevenfold,
    though it costs him all the wealth of his house.
32 But a man who commits adultery lacks judgment;
    whoever does so destroys himself.
33 Blows and disgrace are his lot,
    and his shame will never be wiped away;
34 for jealousy arouses a husband's fury,
    and he will show no mercy when he takes revenge.

35 He will not accept any compensation;
        he will refuse the bribe, however great it is.

DAY 7

Psalm 7
A *shiggaion* [a] of David, which he sang to the Lord
concerning Cush, a Benjamite.

1   O Lord my God, I take refuge in you;
        save and deliver me from all who pursue me,
2   or they will tear me like a lion
        and rip me to pieces with no one to rescue me.

3   O Lord my God, if I have done this
        and there is guilt on my hands—
4   if I have done evil to him who is at peace with me
        or without cause have robbed my foe—
5   then let my enemy pursue and overtake me;
        let him trample my life to the ground
        and make me sleep in the dust.   *Selah*

6   Arise, O Lord, in your anger;
        rise up against the rage of my enemies.
        Awake, my God; decree justice.
7   Let the assembled peoples gather around you.
        Rule over them from on high;
8   let the Lord judge the peoples.
    Judge me, O Lord, according to my righteousness,
        according to my integrity, O Most High.
9   O righteous God,
        who searches minds and hearts,

---

[a] Title: Probably a literary or musical term

DAY 7

bring to an end the violence of the wicked
    and make the righteous secure.
10 My shield *a* is God Most High,
        who saves the upright in heart.
11 God is a righteous judge,
        a God who expresses his wrath every day.
12 If he does not relent,
        he *b* will sharpen his sword;
        he will bend and string his bow.
13 He has prepared his deadly weapons;
        he makes ready his flaming arrows.

14 He who is pregnant with evil
        and conceives trouble gives birth to
            disillusionment.
15 He who digs a hole and scoops it out
        falls into the pit he has made.
16 The trouble he causes recoils on himself;
        his violence comes down on his own head.

17 I will give thanks to the Lord because of his
            righteousness
        and will sing praise to the name of the Lord
            Most High.

Psalm 37 *c*
Of David.

1   Do not fret because of evil men
        or be envious of those who do wrong;

*a*10 Or *sovereign*   *b*12 Or *If a man does not repent, / God*
c This psalm is an acrostic poem, the stanzas of which begin with the
successive letters of the Hebrew alphabet.

2 for like the grass they will soon wither,
   like green plants they will soon die away.

3 Trust in the Lord and do good;
   dwell in the land and enjoy safe pasture.

4 Delight yourself in the Lord
   and he will give you the desires of your heart.

5 Commit your way to the Lord;
   trust in him and he will do this:

6 He will make your righteousness shine like the dawn,
   the justice of your cause like the noonday sun.

7 Be still before the Lord and wait patiently for him;
   do not fret when men succeed in their ways,
   when they carry out their wicked schemes.

8 Refrain from anger and turn from wrath;
   do not fret—it leads only to evil.

9 For evil men will be cut off,
   but those who hope in the Lord will inherit the
   land.

10 A little while, and the wicked will be no more;
   though you look for them, they will not be
   found.

11 But the meek will inherit the land
   and enjoy great peace.

12 The wicked plot against the righteous
   and gnash their teeth at them;

13 but the Lord laughs at the wicked,
   for he knows their day is coming.

14 The wicked draw the sword
   and bend the bow
   to bring down the poor and needy,

to slay those whose ways are upright.
15 But their swords will pierce their own hearts,
    and their bows will be broken.

16 Better the little that the righteous have
    than the wealth of many wicked;
17 for the power of the wicked will be broken,
    but the Lord upholds the righteous.

18 The days of the blameless are known to the Lord,
    and their inheritance will endure forever.
19 In times of disaster they will not wither;
    in days of famine they will enjoy plenty.

20 But the wicked will perish:
    The Lord's enemies will be like the beauty of
        the fields,
    they will vanish—vanish like smoke.

21 The wicked borrow and do not repay,
    but the righteous give generously;
22 those the Lord blesses will inherit the land,
    but those he curses will be cut off.

23 If the Lord delights in a man's way,
    he makes his steps firm;
24 though he stumble, he will not fall,
    for the Lord upholds him with his hand.

25 I was young and now I am old,
    yet I have never seen the righteous forsaken
        or their children begging bread.
26 They are always generous and lend freely;
    their children will be blessed.

27 Turn from evil and do good;
    then you will dwell in the land forever.

28 For the Lord loves the just
   and will not forsake his faithful ones.

   They will be protected forever,
   but the offspring of the wicked will be cut off;
29 the righteous will inherit the land
   and dwell in it forever.

30 The mouth of the righteous man utters wisdom,
   and his tongue speaks what is just.
31 The law of his God is in his heart;
   his feet do not slip.

32 The wicked lie in wait for the righteous,
   seeking their very lives;
33 but the Lord will not leave them in their power
   or let them be condemned when brought to trial.

34 Wait for the Lord
   and keep his way.
   He will exalt you to inherit the land;
   when the wicked are cut off, you will see it.

35 I have seen a wicked and ruthless man
   flourishing like a green tree in its native soil,
36 but he soon passed away and was no more;
   though I looked for him, he could not be found.

37 Consider the blameless, observe the upright;
   there is a future *a* for the man of peace.
38 But all sinners will be destroyed;
   the future *b* of the wicked will be cut off.

39 The salvation of the righteous comes from the Lord;
   he is their stronghold in time of trouble.

---

*a*37 Or *there will be posterity*   *b*38 Or *posterity*

40 The Lord helps them and delivers them;
      he delivers them from the wicked and saves
        them,
      because they take refuge in him.

Psalm 67

For the director of music. With stringed instruments.
A psalm. A song.

1 May God be gracious to us and bless us
      and make his face shine upon us,   *Selah*
2 that your ways may be known on earth,
      your salvation among all nations.

3 May the peoples praise you, O God;
      may all the peoples praise you.
4 May the nations be glad and sing for joy,
      for you rule the peoples justly
      and guide the nations of the earth.   *Selah*
5 May the peoples praise you, O God;
      may all the peoples praise you.

6 Then the land will yield its harvest,
      and God, our God, will bless us.
7 God will bless us,
      and all the ends of the earth will fear him.

Psalm 97

1 The Lord reigns, let the earth be glad;
      let the distant shores rejoice.

2 Clouds and thick darkness surround him;
      righteousness and justice are the foundation
        of his throne.

3 Fire goes before him
    and consumes his foes on every side.
4 His lightning lights up the world;
    the earth sees and trembles.
5 The mountains melt like wax before the Lord,
    before the Lord of all the earth.
6 The heavens proclaim his righteousness,
    and all the peoples see his glory.

7 All who worship images are put to shame,
    those who boast in idols—
    worship him, all you gods!

8 Zion hears and rejoices
    and the villages of Judah are glad
    because of your judgments, O Lord.
9 For you, O Lord, are the Most High over all the
      earth;
    you are exalted far above all gods.

10 Let those who love the Lord hate evil,
    for he guards the lives of his faithful ones
    and delivers them from the hand of the wicked.
11 Light is shed upon the righteous
    and joy on the upright in heart.
12 Rejoice in the Lord, you who are righteous,
    and praise his holy name.

Psalm 127
A song of ascents. Of Solomon.

1 Unless the Lord builds the house,
    its builders labor in vain.
    Unless the Lord watches over the city,
    the watchmen stand guard in vain.

2 In vain you rise early
      and stay up late,
   toiling for food to eat—
      for he grants sleep to *a* those he loves.

3 Sons are a heritage from the Lord,
      children a reward from him.

4 Like arrows in the hands of a warrior
      are sons born in one's youth.

5 Blessed is the man
      whose quiver is full of them.
   They will not be put to shame
      when they contend with their enemies
         in the gate.

Proverbs 7

1 My son, keep my words
      and store up my commands within you.

2 Keep my commands and you will live;
      guard my teachings as the apple of your eye.

3 Bind them on your fingers;
      write them on the tablet of your heart.

4 Say to wisdom, "You are my sister,"
      and call understanding your kinsman;

5 they will keep you from the adulteress,
      from the wayward wife with her seductive
         words.

6 At the window of my house
      I looked out through the lattice.

7 I saw among the simple,
      I noticed among the young men,

a2 Or eat— / for while they sleep he provides for

a youth who lacked judgment.
8   He was going down the street near her corner,
    walking along in the direction of her house
9   at twilight, as the day was fading,
    as the dark of night set in.

10   Then out came a woman to meet him,
    dressed like a prostitute and with
      crafty intent.
11   (She is loud and defiant,
    her feet never stay at home;
12   now in the street, now in the squares,
    at every corner she lurks.)
13   She took hold of him and kissed him
    and with a brazen face she said:

14   "I have fellowship offerings *a* at home;
    today I fulfilled my vows.
15   So I came out to meet you;
    I looked for you and have found you!
16   I have covered my bed
    with colored linens from Egypt.
17   I have perfumed my bed
    with myrrh, aloes and cinnamon.
18   Come, let's drink deep of love till morning;
    let's enjoy ourselves with love!
19   My husband is not at home;
    he has gone on a long journey.
20   He took his purse filled with money
    and will not be home till full moon."

21   With persuasive words she led him astray;
    she seduced him with her smooth talk.

a14 Traditionally *peace offerings*

22 All at once he followed her
        like an ox going to the slaughter,
    like a deer ^a stepping into a noose ^b
23   till an arrow pierces his liver,
    like a bird darting into a snare,
        little knowing it will cost him his life.

24 Now then, my sons, listen to me;
        pay attention to what I say.
25 Do not let your heart turn to her ways
        or stray into her paths.
26 Many are the victims she has brought down;
        her slain are a mighty throng.
27 Her house is a highway to the grave, ^c
        leading down to the chambers of death.

DAY 8

Psalm 8

For the director of music. According to *gittith*. ^d
A psalm of David.

1   O Lord, our Lord,
        how majestic is your name in all the earth!

    You have set your glory
        above the heavens.
2   From the lips of children and infants
        you have ordained praise ^e
    because of your enemies,
        to silence the foe and the avenger.

^a22 Syriac (see also Septuagint); Hebrew *fool*   ^b22 The meaning of
the Hebrew for this line is uncertain.   ^c27 Hebrew *Sheol*
^d Title: Probably a musical term   ^e2 Or *strength*

3 When I consider your heavens,
      the work of your fingers,
   the moon and the stars,
      which you have set in place,
4 what is man that you are mindful of him,
      the son of man that you care for him?
5 You made him a little lower than the heavenly
            beings [a]
      and crowned him with glory and honor.

6 You made him ruler over the works of your hands;
      you put everything under his feet:
7 all flocks and herds,
      and the beasts of the field,
8 the birds of the air,
      and the fish of the sea,
      all that swim the paths of the seas.

9 O Lord, our Lord,
      how majestic is your name in all the earth!

Psalm 38
A psalm of David. A petition.

1 O Lord, do not rebuke me in your anger
      or discipline me in your wrath.
2 For your arrows have pierced me,
      and your hand has come down upon me.
3 Because of your wrath there is no health in my
            body;
      my bones have no soundness because of my sin.
4 My guilt has overwhelmed me
      like a burden too heavy to bear.

[a]5 Or *than God*

5 My wounds fester and are loathsome
      because of my sinful folly.
6 I am bowed down and brought very low;
      all day long I go about mourning.
7 My back is filled with searing pain;
      there is no health in my body.
8 I am feeble and utterly crushed;
      I groan in anguish of heart.

9 All my longings lie open before you, O Lord;
      my sighing is not hidden from you.
10 My heart pounds, my strength fails me;
      even the light has gone from my eyes.
11 My friends and companions avoid me because of
         my wounds;
      my neighbors stay far away.
12 Those who seek my life set their traps,
      those who would harm me talk of my ruin;
      all day long they plot deception.

13 I am like a deaf man, who cannot hear,
      like a mute, who cannot open his mouth;
14 I have become like a man who does not hear,
      whose mouth can offer no reply.
15 I wait for you, O Lord;
      you will answer, O Lord my God.
16 For I said, "Do not let them gloat
      or exalt themselves over me when my foot
         slips."

17 For I am about to fall,
      and my pain is ever with me.
18 I confess my iniquity;
      I am troubled by my sin.
19 Many are those who are my vigorous enemies;

those who hate me without reason are
numerous.
20 Those who repay my good with evil
slander me when I pursue what is good.

21 O Lord, do not forsake me;
be not far from me, O my God.
22 Come quickly to help me,
O Lord my Savior.

Psalm 68

For the director of music. Of David. A psalm. A song.

1 May God arise, may his enemies be scattered;
may his foes flee before him.
2 As smoke is blown away by the wind,
may you blow them away;
as wax melts before the fire,
may the wicked perish before God.
3 But may the righteous be glad
and rejoice before God;
may they be happy and joyful.

4 Sing to God, sing praise to his name,
extol him who rides on the clouds *a*—
his name is the Lord—
and rejoice before him.
5 A father to the fatherless, a defender of widows,
is God in his holy dwelling.
6 God sets the lonely in families, *b*
he leads forth the prisoners with singing;
but the rebellious live in a sun-scorched land.

---

*a*4 Or / prepare the way for him who rides through the deserts
*b*6 Or the desolate in a homeland

7 When you went out before your people, O God,
   when you marched through the
      wasteland,   *Selah*
8   the earth shook,
   the heavens poured down rain,
  before God, the One of Sinai,
   before God, the God of Israel.
9 You gave abundant showers, O God;
   you refreshed your weary inheritance.
10 Your people settled in it,
   and from your bounty, O God, you provided
      for the poor.

11 The Lord announced the word,
   and great was the company of those who
      proclaimed it:
12 "Kings and armies flee in haste;
   in the camps men divide the plunder.
13 Even while you sleep among the campfires, *a*
   the wings of my dove are sheathed with silver,
   its feathers with shining gold."
14 When the Almighty *b* scattered the kings in the
     land,
   it was like snow fallen on Zalmon.

15 The mountains of Bashan are majestic mountains;
   rugged are the mountains of Bashan.
16 Why gaze in envy, O rugged mountains,
   at the mountain where God chooses to reign,
   where the Lord himself will dwell forever?
17 The chariots of God are tens of thousands
   and thousands of thousands;
   the Lord has come from Sinai into his sanctuary.

*a*13 Or *saddlebags*   *b*14 Hebrew *Shaddai*

18 When you ascended on high,
   you led captives in your train;
   you received gifts from men,
even from *a* the rebellious—
   that you, *b* O Lord God, might dwell there.

19 Praise be to the Lord, to God our Savior,
   who daily bears our burdens.   *Selah*
20 Our God is a God who saves;
   from the Sovereign Lord comes escape from
      death.

21 Surely God will crush the heads of his enemies,
   the hairy crowns of those who go on in their
      sins.
22 The Lord says, "I will bring them from Bashan;
   I will bring them from the depths of the sea,
23 that you may plunge your feet in the blood of
      your foes,
   while the tongues of your dogs have their share."

24 Your procession has come into view, O God,
   the procession of my God and King into the
      sanctuary.
25 In front are the singers, after them the musicians;
   with them are the maidens playing
      tambourines.
26 Praise God in the great congregation;
   praise the Lord in the assembly of Israel.
27 There is the little tribe of Benjamin, leading them,
   there the great throng of Judah's princes,
   and there the princes of Zebulun and of
      Naphtali.

*a*18 Or *gifts for men, / even*   *a*18 Or *they*

28 Summon your power, O God *a*;
   show us your strength, O God, as you have
       done before.
29 Because of your temple at Jerusalem
   kings will bring you gifts.
30 Rebuke the beast among the reeds,
   the herd of bulls among the calves of the nations.
   Humbled, may it bring bars of silver.
   Scatter the nations who delight in war.
31 Envoys will come from Egypt;
   Cush *b* will submit herself to God.

32 Sing to God, O kingdoms of the earth,
   sing praise to the Lord,   *Selah*
33 to him who rides the ancient skies above,
   who thunders with mighty voice.
34 Proclaim the power of God,
   whose majesty is over Israel,
   whose power is in the skies.
35 You are awesome, O God, in your sanctuary;
   the God of Israel gives power and strength to
       his people.

   Praise be to God!

Psalm 98
A psalm.

1 Sing to the Lord a new song,
   for he has done marvelous things;
   his right hand and his holy arm

---

*a*28 Many Hebrew manuscripts, Septuagint and Syriac; most Hebrew
manuscripts *Your God has summoned power for you*   *b*31 That is, the
upper Nile region

have worked salvation for him.

2 The Lord has made his salvation known
and revealed his righteousness to the nations.
3 He has remembered his love
and his faithfulness to the house of Israel;
all the ends of the earth have seen
the salvation of our God.

4 Shout for joy to the Lord, all the earth,
burst into jubilant song with music;
5 make music to the Lord with the harp,
with the harp and the sound of singing,
6 with trumpets and the blast of the ram's horn—
shout for joy before the Lord, the King.

7 Let the sea resound, and everything in it,
the world, and all who live in it.
8 Let the rivers clap their hands,
let the mountains sing together for joy;
9 let them sing before the Lord,
for he comes to judge the earth.
He will judge the world in righteousness
and the peoples with equity.

Psalm 128

A song of ascents.

1 Blessed are all who fear the Lord,
who walk in his ways.
2 You will eat the fruit of your labor;
blessings and prosperity will be yours.
3 Your wife will be like a fruitful vine
within your house;
your sons will be like olive shoots
around your table.

4   Thus is the man blessed
        who fears the Lord.

5   May the Lord bless you from Zion
        all the days of your life;
    may you see the prosperity of Jerusalem,
6   and may you live to see your children's children.

    Peace be upon Israel.

Proverbs 8

1   Does not wisdom call out?
        Does not understanding raise her voice?
2   On the heights along the way,
        where the paths meet, she takes her stand;
3   beside the gates leading into the city,
        at the entrances, she cries aloud:
4   "To you, O men, I call out;
        I raise my voice to all mankind.
5   You who are simple, gain prudence;
        you who are foolish, gain understanding.
6   Listen, for I have worthy things to say;
        I open my lips to speak what is right.
7   My mouth speaks what is true,
        for my lips detest wickedness.
8   All the words of my mouth are just;
        none of them is crooked or perverse.
9   To the discerning all of them are right;
        they are faultless to those who have knowledge.
10   Choose my instruction instead of silver,
        knowledge rather than choice gold,
11   for wisdom is more precious than rubies,
        and nothing you desire can compare with her.

12 "I, wisdom, dwell together with prudence;
  I possess knowledge and discretion.
13 To fear the Lord is to hate evil;
  I hate pride and arrogance,
    evil behavior and perverse speech.
14 Counsel and sound judgment are mine;
  I have understanding and power.
15 By me kings reign
  and rulers make laws that are just;
16 by me princes govern,
  and all nobles who rule on earth. *a*
17 I love those who love me,
  and those who seek me find me.
18 With me are riches and honor,
  enduring wealth and prosperity.
19 My fruit is better than fine gold;
  what I yield surpasses choice silver.
20 I walk in the way of righteousness,
  along the paths of justice,
21 bestowing wealth on those who love me
  and making their treasuries full.

22 "The Lord brought me forth *b* as the first of his
      works *c*,
  before his deeds of old;
23 I was appointed *d* from eternity,
  from the beginning, before the world began.
24 When there were no oceans, I was given birth,
  when there were no springs abounding with
      water;

---

a16 Many Hebrew manuscripts and Septuagint; most Hebrew
manuscripts and nobles—*all righteous rulers* *b22* Or *The Lord
possessed me* *c22* Or *way;* or *dominion* *d23* Or *fashioned*

25 before the mountains were settled in place,
    before the hills, I was given birth,
26 before he made the earth or its fields
    or any of the dust of the world.
27 I was there when he set the heavens in place,
    when he marked out the horizon on the face of
      the deep,
28 when he established the clouds above
    and fixed securely the fountains of the deep,
29 when he gave the sea its boundary
    so the waters would not overstep his command,
  and when he marked out the foundations of the
      earth.
30   Then I was the craftsman at his side.
  I was filled with delight day after day,
    rejoicing always in his presence,
31 rejoicing in his whole world
    and delighting in mankind.

32 "Now then, my sons, listen to me;
    blessed are those who keep my ways.
33 Listen to my instruction and be wise;
    do not ignore it.
34 Blessed is the man who listens to me,
    watching daily at my doors,
    waiting at my doorway.
35 For whoever finds me finds life
    and receives favor from the Lord.
36 But whoever fails to find me harms himself;
    all who hate me love death."

DAY 9

Psalm 9 [a]
For the director of music. To the tune of
"The Death of the Son." A psalm of David.

1 I will praise you, O Lord, with all my heart;
     I will tell of all your wonders.
2 I will be glad and rejoice in you;
     I will sing praise to your name, O Most High.

3 My enemies turn back;
     they stumble and perish before you.
4 For you have upheld my right and my cause;
     you have sat on your throne, judging righteously.
5 You have rebuked the nations and destroyed the
          wicked;
     you have blotted out their name for ever and ever.
6 Endless ruin has overtaken the enemy,
     you have uprooted their cities;
     even the memory of them has perished.

7 The Lord reigns forever;
     he has established his throne for judgment.
8 He will judge the world in righteousness;
     he will govern the peoples with justice.
9 The Lord is a refuge for the oppressed,
     a stronghold in times of trouble.
10 Those who know your name will trust in you,
     for you, Lord, have never forsaken those who
          seek you.

---

[a] Psalms 9 and 10 may have been originally a single acrostic poem,
the stanzas of which begin with the successive letters of the Hebrew
alphabet. In the Septuagint they constitute one psalm.

11 Sing praises to the Lord, enthroned in Zion;
        proclaim among the nations what he has done.
12 For he who avenges blood remembers;
        he does not ignore the cry of the afflicted.

13 O Lord, see how my enemies persecute me!
        Have mercy and lift me up from the gates of
            death,
14 that I may declare your praises
        in the gates of the Daughter of Zion
        and there rejoice in your salvation.
15 The nations have fallen into the pit they have dug;
        their feet are caught in the net they have hidden.
16 The Lord is known by his justice;
        the wicked are ensnared by the
            work of their hands.   *Higgaion.* [a] *Selah*

17 The wicked return to the grave, [b]
        all the nations that forget God.
18 But the needy will not always be forgotten,
        nor the hope of the afflicted ever perish.

19 Arise, O Lord, let not man triumph;
        let the nations be judged in your presence.
20 Strike them with terror, O Lord;
        let the nations know they are but men.   *Selah*

Psalm 39
For the director of music. For Jeduthun.
A psalm of David.

1 I said, "I will watch my ways
        and keep my tongue from sin;

---

[a]16 Or *Meditation;* possibly a musical notation   [b]17 Hebrew *Sheol*

I will put a muzzle on my mouth
 as long as the wicked are in my presence."
2 But when I was silent and still,
 not even saying anything good,
 my anguish increased.
3 My heart grew hot within me,
 and as I meditated, the fire burned;
 then I spoke with my tongue:

4 "Show me, O Lord, my life's end
 and the number of my days;
 let me know how fleeting is my life.
5 You have made my days a mere handbreadth;
 the span of my years is as nothing before you.
 Each man's life is but a breath.   *Selah*
6 Man is a mere phantom as he goes to and fro:
 He bustles about, but only in vain;
 he heaps up wealth, not knowing who will get
  it.

7 But now, Lord, what do I look for?
 My hope is in you.
8 Save me from all my transgressions;
 do not make me the scorn of fools.
9 I was silent; I would not open my mouth,
 for you are the one who has done this.
10 Remove your scourge from me;
 I am overcome by the blow of your hand.
11 You rebuke and discipline men for their sin;
 you consume their wealth like a moth—
 each man is but a breath.   *Selah*

12 Hear my prayer, O Lord,
 listen to my cry for help;
 be not deaf to my weeping.

    For I dwell with you as an alien,
      a stranger, as all my fathers were.
13 Look away from me, that I may rejoice again
      before I depart and am no more."

Psalm 69

For the director of music. To the tune of "Lilies."
Of David.

1 Save me, O God,
    for the waters have come up to my neck.
2 I sink in the miry depths,
    where there is no foothold.
I have come into the deep waters;
    the floods engulf me.
3 I am worn out calling for help;
    my throat is parched.
My eyes fail,
    looking for my God.
4 Those who hate me without reason
    outnumber the hairs of my head;
many are my enemies without cause,
    those who seek to destroy me.
I am forced to restore
    what I did not steal.

5 You know my folly, O God;
    my guilt is not hidden from you.

6 May those who hope in you
    not be disgraced because of me,
    O Lord, the Lord Almighty;
may those who seek you
    not be put to shame because of me,
    O God of Israel.

7   For I endure scorn for your sake,
      and shame covers my face.
8   I am a stranger to my brothers,
      an alien to my own mother's sons;
9   for zeal for your house consumes me,
      and the insults of those who insult you fall on me.
10 When I weep and fast,
      I must endure scorn;
11 when I put on sackcloth,
      people make sport of me.
12 Those who sit at the gate mock me,
      and I am the song of the drunkards.

13 But I pray to you, O Lord,
      in the time of your favor;
    in your great love, O God,
      answer me with your sure salvation.
14 Rescue me from the mire,
      do not let me sink;
    deliver me from those who hate me,
      from the deep waters.
15 Do not let the floodwaters engulf me
      or the depths swallow me up
      or the pit close its mouth over me.
16 Answer me, O Lord, out of the goodness of your
        love;
      in your great mercy turn to me.
17 Do not hide your face from your servant;
      answer me quickly, for I am in trouble.
18 Come near and rescue me;
      redeem me because of my foes.

19 You know how I am scorned, disgraced and
        shamed;
      all my enemies are before you.

20 Scorn has broken my heart
        and has left me helpless;
    I looked for sympathy, but there was none,
        for comforters, but I found none.
21 They put gall in my food
        and gave me vinegar for my thirst.

22 May the table set before them become a snare;
        may it become retribution and *a* a trap.
23 May their eyes be darkened so they cannot see,
        and their backs be bent forever.
24 Pour out your wrath on them;
        let your fierce anger overtake them.
25 May their place be deserted;
        let there be no one to dwell in their tents.
26 For they persecute those you wound
        and talk about the pain of those you hurt.
27 Charge them with crime upon crime;
        do not let them share in your salvation.
28 May they be blotted out of the book of life
        and not be listed with the righteous.

29 I am in pain and distress;
        may your salvation, O God, protect me.

30 I will praise God's name in song
        and glorify him with thanksgiving.
31 This will please the Lord more than an ox,
        more than a bull with its horns and hoofs.
32 The poor will see and be glad—
        you who seek God, may your hearts live!
33 The Lord hears the needy
        and does not despise his captive people.

---

*a*22 Or *snare / and their fellowship become*

34 Let heaven and earth praise him,
    the seas and all that move in them,
35 for God will save Zion
    and rebuild the cities of Judah.
   Then people will settle there and possess it;
36   the children of his servants will inherit it,
    and those who love his name will dwell there.

Psalm 99

1 The Lord reigns,
    let the nations tremble;
   he sits enthroned between the cherubim,
    let the earth shake.
2 Great is the Lord in Zion;
    he is exalted over all the nations.
3 Let them praise your great and awesome name—
    he is holy.

4 The King is mighty, he loves justice—
    you have established equity;
   in Jacob you have done
    what is just and right.
5 Exalt the Lord our God
    and worship at his footstool;
    he is holy.

6 Moses and Aaron were among his priests,
    Samuel was among those who called on his
        name;
   they called on the Lord
    and he answered them.
7 He spoke to them from the pillar of cloud;
    they kept his statutes and the decrees he gave
        them.

8   O Lord our God,
        you answered them;
    you were to Israel *a* a forgiving God,
        though you punished their misdeeds. *b*

9   Exalt the Lord our God
        and worship at his holy mountain,
        for the Lord our God is holy.

Psalm 129

A song of ascents.

1   They have greatly oppressed me from my youth—
        let Israel say—

2   they have greatly oppressed me from my youth,
        but they have not gained the victory over me.

3   Plowmen have plowed my back
        and made their furrows long.

4   But the Lord is righteous;
        he has cut me free from the cords of the wicked.

5   May all who hate Zion
        be turned back in shame.

6   May they be like grass on the roof,
        which withers before it can grow;

7   with it the reaper cannot fill his hands,
        nor the one who gathers fill his arms.

8   May those who pass by not say,
        "The blessing of the Lord be upon you;
        we bless you in the name of the Lord."

---

*a*8 Hebrew *them*   *b*8 Or / *an avenger of the wrongs done to them*

Proverbs 9

1 Wisdom has built her house;
    she has hewn out its seven pillars.
2 She has prepared her meat and mixed her
    wine;
    she has also set her table.
3 She has sent out her maids, and she calls
    from the highest point of the city.
4 "Let all who are simple come in here!"
    she says to those who lack judgment.
5 "Come, eat my food
    and drink the wine I have mixed.
6 Leave your simple ways and you will live;
    walk in the way of understanding.

7 "Whoever corrects a mocker invites insult;
    whoever rebukes a wicked man incurs abuse.
8 Do not rebuke a mocker or he will hate you;
    rebuke a wise man and he will love you.
9 Instruct a wise man and he will be wiser still;
    teach a righteous man and he will add to his
    learning.

10 "The fear of the Lord is the beginning of wisdom,
    and knowledge of the Holy One is
    understanding.
11 For through me your days will be many,
    and years will be added to your life.
12 If you are wise, your wisdom will reward you;
    if you are a mocker, you alone will suffer."

13 The woman Folly is loud;
    she is undisciplined and without knowledge.
14 She sits at the door of her house,
    on a seat at the highest point of the city,

15   calling out to those who pass by,
        who go straight on their way.
16   "Let all who are simple come in here!"
        she says to those who lack judgment.
17   "Stolen water is sweet;
        food eaten in secret is delicious!"
18   But little do they know that the dead are there,
        that her guests are in the depths of the grave. [a]

DAY 10

Psalm 10 [b]

1   Why, O Lord, do you stand far off?
        Why do you hide yourself in times of trouble?

2   In his arrogance the wicked man hunts down the
        weak,
        who are caught in the schemes he devises.
3   He boasts of the cravings of his heart;
        he blesses the greedy and reviles the Lord.
4   In his pride the wicked does not seek him;
        in all his thoughts there is no room for God.
5   His ways are always prosperous;
        he is haughty and your laws are far from him;
        he sneers at all his enemies.
6   He says to himself, "Nothing will shake me;
        I'll always be happy and never have trouble."
7   His mouth is full of curses and lies and threats;

---

[a]18 Hebrew *Sheol*   [b] Psalms 9 and 10 may have been originally a single acrostic poem, the stanzas of which begin with the successive letters of the Hebrew alphabet. In the Septuagint they constitute one psalm.

trouble and evil are under his tongue.
8 He lies in wait near the villages;
from ambush he murders the innocent,
watching in secret for his victims.
9 He lies in wait like a lion in cover;
he lies in wait to catch the helpless;
he catches the helpless and drags them off in
his net.
10 His victims are crushed, they collapse;
they fall under his strength.
11 He says to himself, "God has forgotten;
he covers his face and never sees."

12 Arise, Lord! Lift up your hand, O God.
Do not forget the helpless.
13 Why does the wicked man revile God?
Why does he say to himself,
"He won't call me to account"?
14 But you, O God, do see trouble and grief;
you consider it to take it in hand.
The victim commits himself to you;
you are the helper of the fatherless.
15 Break the arm of the wicked and evil man;
call him to account for his wickedness
that would not be found out.

16 The Lord is King for ever and ever;
the nations will perish from his land.
17 You hear, O Lord, the desire of the afflicted;
you encourage them, and you listen to
their cry,
18 defending the fatherless and the oppressed,
in order that man, who is of the earth, may
terrify no more.

Psalm 40

For the director of music. Of David. A psalm.

1 I waited patiently for the Lord;
   he turned to me and heard my cry.
2 He lifted me out of the slimy pit,
   out of the mud and mire;
   he set my feet on a rock
   and gave me a firm place to stand.
3 He put a new song in my mouth,
   a hymn of praise to our God.
   Many will see and fear
   and put their trust in the Lord.

4 Blessed is the man
   who makes the Lord his trust,
   who does not look to the proud,
   to those who turn aside to false gods. *a*
5 Many, O Lord my God,
   are the wonders you have done.
   The things you planned for us
   no one can recount to you;
   were I to speak and tell of them,
   they would be too many to declare.

6 Sacrifice and offering you did not desire,
   but my ears you have pierced *b c*;
   burnt offerings and sin offerings
   you did not require.
7 Then I said, "Here I am, I have come—
   it is written about me in the scroll. *a*

---

a4 Or *to falsehood*   *b6* Hebrew; Septuagint *but a body you have
prepared for me* (see also Symmachus and Theodotion)   *c6* Or *opened*
d7 Or *come / with the scroll written for me*

8   I desire to do your will, O my God;
        your law is within my heart."

9   I proclaim righteousness in the great assembly;
        I do not seal my lips,
        as you know, O Lord.
10 I do not hide your righteousness in my heart;
        I speak of your faithfulness and salvation.
    I do not conceal your love and your truth
        from the great assembly.

11 Do not withhold your mercy from me, O Lord;
        may your love and your truth always protect
            me.
12 For troubles without number surround me;
        my sins have overtaken me, and I cannot see.
    They are more than the hairs of my head,
        and my heart fails within me.

13 Be pleased, O Lord, to save me;
        O Lord, come quickly to help me.
14 May all who seek to take my life
        be put to shame and confusion;
    may all who desire my ruin
        be turned back in disgrace.
15 May those who say to me, "Aha! Aha!"
        be appalled at their own shame.
16 But may all who seek you
        rejoice and be glad in you;
    may those who love your salvation always say,
        "The Lord be exalted!"

17 Yet I am poor and needy;
        may the Lord think of me.
    You are my help and my deliverer;
        O my God, do not delay.

Psalm 70

For the director of music. Of David. A petition.

1   Hasten, O God, to save me;
    O Lord, come quickly to help me.
2   May those who seek my life
    be put to shame and confusion;
    may all who desire my ruin
    be turned back in disgrace.
3   May those who say to me, "Aha! Aha!"
    turn back because of their shame.
4   But may all who seek you
    rejoice and be glad in you;
    may those who love your salvation always say,
    "Let God be exalted!"

5   Yet I am poor and needy;
    come quickly to me, O God.
    You are my help and my deliverer;
    O Lord, do not delay.

Psalm 100

A psalm. For giving thanks.

1   Shout for joy to the Lord, all the earth.
2   Worship the Lord with gladness;
    come before him with joyful songs.
3   Know that the Lord is God.
    It is he who made us, and we are his [a];
    we are his people, the sheep of his pasture.

4   Enter his gates with thanksgiving
    and his courts with praise;

[a]3 Or *and not we ourselves*

give thanks to him and praise his name.
5 For the Lord is good and his love endures forever;
   his faithfulness continues through all
      generations.

Psalm 130
A song of ascents.

1 Out of the depths I cry to you, O Lord;
2   O Lord, hear my voice.
   Let your ears be attentive
      to my cry for mercy.

3 If you, O Lord, kept a record of sins,
   O Lord, who could stand?
4 But with you there is forgiveness;
   therefore you are feared.

5 I wait for the Lord, my soul waits,
   and in his word I put my hope.
6 My soul waits for the Lord
   more than watchmen wait for the morning,
   more than watchmen wait for the morning.

7 O Israel, put your hope in the Lord,
   for with the Lord is unfailing love
   and with him is full redemption.
8 He himself will redeem Israel
   from all their sins.

Proverbs 10
1 The proverbs of Solomon:

   A wise son brings joy to his father,
      but a foolish son grief to his mother.

2   Ill-gotten treasures are of no value,
        but righteousness delivers from death.

3   The Lord does not let the righteous go hungry
        but he thwarts the craving of the wicked.

4   Lazy hands make a man poor,
        but diligent hands bring wealth.

5   He who gathers crops in summer is a wise son,
        but he who sleeps during harvest is a
            disgraceful son.

6   Blessings crown the head of the righteous,
        but violence overwhelms the mouth of the
            wicked. *a*

7   The memory of the righteous will be a blessing,
        but the name of the wicked will rot.

8   The wise in heart accept commands,
        but a chattering fool comes to ruin.

9   The man of integrity walks securely,
        but he who takes crooked paths will be found
            out.

10 He who winks maliciously causes grief,
        and a chattering fool comes to ruin.

11 The mouth of the righteous is a fountain of life,
        but violence overwhelms the mouth of the
            wicked.

12 Hatred stirs up dissension,
        but love covers over all wrongs.

---

a6 Or *but the mouth of the wicked conceals violence*; also in verse 11

13 Wisdom is found on the lips of the discerning,
   but a rod is for the back of him who lacks
   judgment.

14 Wise men store up knowledge,
   but the mouth of a fool invites ruin.

15 The wealth of the rich is their fortified city,
   but poverty is the ruin of the poor.

16 The wages of the righteous bring them life,
   but the income of the wicked brings them
   punishment.

17 He who heeds discipline shows the way to life,
   but whoever ignores correction leads others
   astray.

18 He who conceals his hatred has lying lips,
   and whoever spreads slander is a fool.

19 When words are many, sin is not absent,
   but he who holds his tongue is wise.

20 The tongue of the righteous is choice silver,
   but the heart of the wicked is of little value.

21 The lips of the righteous nourish many,
   but fools die for lack of judgment.

22 The blessing of the Lord brings wealth,
   and he adds no trouble to it.

23 A fool finds pleasure in evil conduct,
   but a man of understanding delights in
   wisdom.

24 What the wicked dreads will overtake him;
   what the righteous desire will be granted.

25 When the storm has swept by, the wicked are
       gone,
   but the righteous stand firm forever.

26 As vinegar to the teeth and smoke to the eyes,
   so is a sluggard to those who send him.

27 The fear of the Lord adds length to life,
   but the years of the wicked are cut short.

28 The prospect of the righteous is joy,
   but the hopes of the wicked come to nothing.

29 The way of the Lord is a refuge for the
       righteous,
   but it is the ruin of those who do evil.

30 The righteous will never be uprooted,
   but the wicked will not remain in the land.

31 The mouth of the righteous brings forth wisdom,
   but a perverse tongue will be cut out.

32 The lips of the righteous know what is fitting,
   but the mouth of the wicked only what is
       perverse.

DAY 11

Psalm 11
For the director of music. Of David.

1 In the Lord I take refuge.
   How then can you say to me:
   "Flee like a bird to your mountain.
2 For look, the wicked bend their bows;
   they set their arrows against the strings

    to shoot from the shadows
      at the upright in heart.
3   When the foundations are being destroyed,
      what can the righteous do [a]?"

4   The Lord is in his holy temple;
      the Lord is on his heavenly throne.
    He observes the sons of men;
      his eyes examine them.
5   The Lord examines the righteous,
      but the wicked [b] and those who love violence
      his soul hates.
6   On the wicked he will rain
      fiery coals and burning sulfur;
      a scorching wind will be their lot.

7   For the Lord is righteous,
      he loves justice;
      upright men will see his face.

Psalm 41

For the director of music. A psalm of David.

1   Blessed is he who has regard for the weak;
      the Lord delivers him in times of trouble.
2   The Lord will protect him and preserve his life;
      he will bless him in the land
      and not surrender him to the desire of
        his foes.
3   The Lord will sustain him on his sickbed
      and restore him from his bed of illness.

[a]3 Or *what is the Righteous One doing*   [b]5 Or *The Lord, the Righteous One, examines the wicked, /*

4 I said, "O Lord, have mercy on me;
     heal me, for I have sinned against you."
5 My enemies say of me in malice,
     "When will he die and his name perish?"
6 Whenever one comes to see me,
     he speaks falsely, while his heart gathers
        slander;
     then he goes out and spreads it abroad.

7 All my enemies whisper together against me;
     they imagine the worst for me, saying,
8 "A vile disease has beset him;
     he will never get up from the place where
        he lies."
9 Even my close friend, whom I trusted,
     he who shared my bread,
     has lifted up his heel against me.

10 But you, O Lord, have mercy on me;
      raise me up, that I may repay them.
11 I know that you are pleased with me,
      for my enemy does not triumph over me.
12 In my integrity you uphold me
      and set me in your presence forever.

13 Praise be to the Lord, the God of Israel,
      from everlasting to everlasting.
                    Amen and Amen.

Psalm 71

1 In you, O Lord, I have taken refuge;
     let me never be put to shame.
2 Rescue me and deliver me in your righteousness;
     turn your ear to me and save me.

3 Be my rock of refuge,
       to which I can always go;
   give the command to save me,
       for you are my rock and my fortress.
4 Deliver me, O my God, from the hand of the
       wicked,
       from the grasp of evil and cruel men.

5 For you have been my hope, O Sovereign Lord,
       my confidence since my youth.
6 From birth I have relied on you;
       you brought me forth from my mother's womb.
       I will ever praise you.
7 I have become like a portent to many,
       but you are my strong refuge.
8 My mouth is filled with your praise,
       declaring your splendor all day long.

9 Do not cast me away when I am old;
       do not forsake me when my strength is gone.
10 For my enemies speak against me;
       those who wait to kill me conspire together.
11 They say, "God has forsaken him;
       pursue him and seize him,
       for no one will rescue him."
12 Be not far from me, O God;
       come quickly, O my God, to help me.
13 May my accusers perish in shame;
       may those who want to harm me
       be covered with scorn and disgrace.

14 But as for me, I will always have hope;
       I will praise you more and more.
15 My mouth will tell of your righteousness,
       of your salvation all day long,

> though I know not its measure.
> 16 I will come and proclaim your mighty acts,
>   O Sovereign Lord;
> I will proclaim your righteousness,
>   yours alone.
> 17 Since my youth, O God, you have taught me,
>   and to this day I declare your marvelous deeds.
> 18 Even when I am old and gray,
>   do not forsake me, O God,
> till I declare your power to the next generation,
>   your might to all who are to come.
>
> 19 Your righteousness reaches to the skies, O God,
>   you who have done great things.
>   Who, O God, is like you?
> 20 Though you have made me see troubles,
>   many and bitter,
>   you will restore my life again;
> from the depths of the earth
>   you will again bring me up.
> 21 You will increase my honor
>   and comfort me once again.
> 22 I will praise you with the harp
>   for your faithfulness, O my God;
> I will sing praise to you with the lyre,
>   O Holy One of Israel.
> 23 My lips will shout for joy
>   when I sing praise to you—
>   I, whom you have redeemed.
> 24 My tongue will tell of your righteous acts
>   all day long,
> for those who wanted to harm me
>   have been put to shame and confusion.

Psalm 101

Of David. A psalm.

1   I will sing of your love and justice;
       to you, O Lord, I will sing praise.
2   I will be careful to lead a blameless life—
       when will you come to me?

     I will walk in my house
       with blameless heart.
3   I will set before my eyes
       no vile thing.

     The deeds of faithless men I hate;
       they will not cling to me.
4   Men of perverse heart shall be far from me;
       I will have nothing to do with evil.

5   Whoever slanders his neighbor in secret,
       him will I put to silence;
     whoever has haughty eyes and a proud heart,
       him will I not endure.

6   My eyes will be on the faithful in the land,
       that they may dwell with me;
     he whose walk is blameless
       will minister to me.

7   No one who practices deceit
       will dwell in my house;
     no one who speaks falsely
       will stand in my presence.

8   Every morning I will put to silence
       all the wicked in the land;
     I will cut off every evildoer
       from the city of the Lord.

Psalm 131

A song of ascents. Of David.

1   My heart is not proud, O Lord,
        my eyes are not haughty;
    I do not concern myself with great matters
        or things too wonderful for me.

2   But I have stilled and quieted my soul;
        like a weaned child with its mother,
        like a weaned child is my soul within me.

3   O Israel, put your hope in the Lord
        both now and forevermore.

Proverbs 11

1   The Lord abhors dishonest scales,
        but accurate weights are his delight.

2   When pride comes, then comes disgrace,
        but with humility comes wisdom.

3   The integrity of the upright guides them,
        but the unfaithful are destroyed by their
            duplicity.

4   Wealth is worthless in the day of wrath,
        but righteousness delivers from death.

5   The righteousness of the blameless makes a
            straight way for them,
        but the wicked are brought down by
            their own wickedness.

6   The righteousness of the upright delivers them,
        but the unfaithful are trapped by evil
            desires.

7 When a wicked man dies, his hope perishes;
   all he expected from his power comes to nothing.

8 The righteous man is rescued from trouble,
   and it comes on the wicked instead.

9 With his mouth the godless destroys his neighbor,
   but through knowledge the righteous
      escape.

10 When the righteous prosper, the city rejoices;
   when the wicked perish, there are shouts of joy.

11 Through the blessing of the upright a city is exalted,
   but by the mouth of the wicked it is destroyed.

12 A man who lacks judgment derides his neighbor,
   but a man of understanding holds his tongue.

13 A gossip betrays a confidence,
   but a trustworthy man keeps a secret.

14 For lack of guidance a nation falls,
   but many advisers make victory sure.

15 He who puts up security for another will surely
      suffer,
   but whoever refuses to strike hands in pledge is
      safe.

16 A kindhearted woman gains respect,
   but ruthless men gain only wealth.

17 A kind man benefits himself,
   but a cruel man brings trouble on himself.

18 The wicked man earns deceptive wages,
   but he who sows righteousness reaps a sure
      reward.

19 The truly righteous man attains life,
    but he who pursues evil goes to his death.

20 The Lord detests men of perverse heart
    but he delights in those whose ways are
        blameless.

21 Be sure of this: The wicked will not go unpunished,
    but those who are righteous will go free.

22 Like a gold ring in a pig's snout
    is a beautiful woman who shows no discretion.

23 The desire of the righteous ends only in good,
    but the hope of the wicked only in wrath.

24 One man gives freely, yet gains even more;
    another withholds unduly, but comes to poverty.

25 A generous man will prosper;
    he who refreshes others will himself be refreshed.

26 People curse the man who hoards grain,
    but blessing crowns him who is willing to sell.

27 He who seeks good finds goodwill,
    but evil comes to him who searches for it.

28 Whoever trusts in his riches will fall,
    but the righteous will thrive like a green leaf.

29 He who brings trouble on his family will inherit
      only wind,
    and the fool will be servant to the wise.

30 The fruit of the righteous is a tree of life,
    and he who wins souls is wise.

31 If the righteous receive their due on earth,
    how much more the ungodly and the sinner!

DAY 12

Psalm 12

For the director of music. According to *sheminith*. [a]
A psalm of David.

1   Help, Lord, for the godly are no more;
        the faithful have vanished from among men.

2   Everyone lies to his neighbor;
        their flattering lips speak with deception.

3   May the Lord cut off all flattering lips
        and every boastful tongue

4   that says, "We will triumph with our tongues;
        we own our lips [b]—who is our master?"

5   "Because of the oppression of the weak
        and the groaning of the needy,
    I will now arise," says the Lord.
        "I will protect them from those who
            malign them."

6   And the words of the Lord are flawless,
        like silver refined in a furnace
            of clay,
        purified seven times.

7   O Lord, you will keep us safe
        and protect us from such people
            forever.

8   The wicked freely strut about
        when what is vile is honored
            among men.

---

[a] Title: Probably a musical term   [b] 4 Or / our lips are our plowshares

Psalm 42 [a]

For the director of music. A *maskil* [b]
of the Sons of Korah.

1 As the deer pants for streams of water,
    so my soul pants for you, O God.
2 My soul thirsts for God, for the living God.
    When can I go and meet with God?
3 My tears have been my food
    day and night,
while men say to me all day long,
    "Where is your God?"
4 These things I remember
    as I pour out my soul:
how I used to go with the multitude,
    leading the procession to the house of God,
with shouts of joy and thanksgiving
    among the festive throng.

5 Why are you downcast, O my soul?
    Why so disturbed within me?
Put your hope in God,
    for I will yet praise him,
    my Savior and 6 my God.

My [c] soul is downcast within me;
    therefore I will remember you
from the land of the Jordan,
    the heights of Hermon—
      from Mount Mizar.

[a] In many Hebrew manuscripts Psalms 42 and 43 constitute one
psalm.   [b] Title: Probably a literary or musical term   [c] 5,6 A few
Hebrew manuscripts, Septuagint and Syriac; most Hebrew
manuscripts *praise him for his saving help.* / 6 *O my God, my*

7   Deep calls to deep
        in the roar of your waterfalls;
    all your waves and breakers
        have swept over me.

8   By day the Lord directs his love,
        at night his song is with me—
        a prayer to the God of my life.

9   I say to God my Rock,
        "Why have you forgotten me?
    Why must I go about mourning,
        oppressed by the enemy?"
10 My bones suffer mortal agony
        as my foes taunt me,
    saying to me all day long,
        "Where is your God?"

11 Why are you downcast, O my soul?
        Why so disturbed within me?
    Put your hope in God,
        for I will yet praise him,
        my Savior and my God.

Psalm 72
Of Solomon.

1   Endow the king with your justice, O God,
        the royal son with your righteousness.
2   He will *a* judge your people in righteousness,
        your afflicted ones with justice.
3   The mountains will bring prosperity to the people,
        the hills the fruit of righteousness.

---

a 2 Or *May he;* similarly in verses 3-11 and 17

4 He will defend the afflicted among the people
   and save the children of the needy;
   he will crush the oppressor.

5 He will endure *a* as long as the sun,
   as long as the moon, through all generations.
6 He will be like rain falling on a mown field,
   like showers watering the earth.
7 In his days the righteous will flourish;
   prosperity will abound till the moon is no more.

8 He will rule from sea to sea
   and from the River *b* to the ends of the earth. *c*
9 The desert tribes will bow before him
   and his enemies will lick the dust.
10 The kings of Tarshish and of distant shores
    will bring tribute to him;
    the kings of Sheba and Seba
    will present him gifts.
11 All kings will bow down to him
    and all nations will serve him.

12 For he will deliver the needy who cry out,
    the afflicted who have no one to help.
13 He will take pity on the weak and the needy
    and save the needy from death.
14 He will rescue them from oppression and violence,
    for precious is their blood in his sight.
15 Long may he live!
    May gold from Sheba be given him.
    May people ever pray for him
    and bless him all day long.

---

*a*5 Septuagint; Hebrew *You will be feared*   *b*8 That is, the Euphrates
*c*8 Or *the end of the land*

16 Let grain abound throughout the land;
     on the tops of the hills may it sway.
   Let its fruit flourish like Lebanon;
     let it thrive like the grass of the field.
17 May his name endure forever;
     may it continue as long as the sun.
   All nations will be blessed through him,
     and they will call him blessed.

18 Praise be to the Lord God, the God of Israel,
     who alone does marvelous deeds.
19 Praise be to his glorious name forever;
     may the whole earth be filled with his glory.
                    Amen and Amen.

20 This concludes the prayers of David son of Jesse.

Psalm 102

A prayer of an afflicted man. When he is faint
and pours out his lament before the Lord.

1 Hear my prayer, O Lord;
    let my cry for help come to you.
2 Do not hide your face from me
    when I am in distress.
  Turn your ear to me;
    when I call, answer me quickly.

3 For my days vanish like smoke;
    my bones burn like glowing embers.
4 My heart is blighted and withered like grass;
    I forget to eat my food.
5 Because of my loud groaning
    I am reduced to skin and bones.
6 I am like a desert owl,

like an owl among the ruins.
7 I lie awake; I have become
like a bird alone on a roof.
8 All day long my enemies taunt me;
those who rail against me use my name as a curse.
9 For I eat ashes as my food
and mingle my drink with tears
10 because of your great wrath,
for you have taken me up and thrown me aside.
11 My days are like the evening shadow;
I wither away like grass.

12 But you, O Lord, sit enthroned forever;
your renown endures through all generations.
13 You will arise and have compassion on Zion,
for it is time to show favor to her;
the appointed time has come.
14 For her stones are dear to your servants;
her very dust moves them to pity.
15 The nations will fear the name of the Lord,
all the kings of the earth will revere your glory.
16 For the Lord will rebuild Zion
and appear in his glory.
17 He will respond to the prayer of the destitute;
he will not despise their plea.

18 Let this be written for a future generation,
that a people not yet created may praise the Lord:
19 "The Lord looked down from his sanctuary on
high,
from heaven he viewed the earth,
20 to hear the groans of the prisoners
and release those condemned to death."
21 So the name of the Lord will be declared in Zion
and his praise in Jerusalem

22 when the peoples and the kingdoms
        assemble to worship the Lord.

23 In the course of my life [a] he broke my strength;
        he cut short my days.
24 So I said:
        "Do not take me away, O my God, in the midst
            of my days;
        your years go on through all generations.
25 In the beginning you laid the foundations of the
            earth,
        and the heavens are the work of your hands.
26 They will perish, but you remain;
        they will all wear out like a garment.
    Like clothing you will change them
        and they will be discarded.
27 But you remain the same,
        and your years will never end.
28 The children of your servants will live in your
            presence;
        their descendants will be established before
            you."

Psalm 132

A song of ascents.

1   O Lord, remember David
        and all the hardships he endured.

2   He swore an oath to the Lord
        and made a vow to the Mighty One of Jacob:
3   "I will not enter my house
        or go to my bed—

---

[a] 23 Or *By his power*

4   I will allow no sleep to my eyes,
     no slumber to my eyelids,

5   till I find a place for the Lord,
     a dwelling for the Mighty One of Jacob."

6   We heard it in Ephrathah,
     we came upon it in the fields of Jaar *a: b*

7   "Let us go to his dwelling place;
     let us worship at his footstool—

8   arise, O Lord, and come to your resting place,
     you and the ark of your might.

9   May your priests be clothed with righteousness;
     may your saints sing for joy."

10   For the sake of David your servant,
     do not reject your anointed one.

11   The Lord swore an oath to David,
     a sure oath that he will not revoke:
   "One of your own descendants
     I will place on your throne—

12   if your sons keep my covenant
     and the statutes I teach them,
   then their sons will sit
     on your throne for ever and ever."

13   For the Lord has chosen Zion,
     he has desired it for his dwelling:

14   "This is my resting place for ever and ever;
     here I will sit enthroned, for I have desired it—

15   I will bless her with abundant provisions;
     her poor will I satisfy with food.

---

a6 That is, Kiriath Jearim   *b6* Or *heard of it in Ephrathah, / we found it in the fields of Jaar.* (And no quotes around verses 7-9)

16 I will clothe her priests with salvation,
        and her saints will ever sing for joy.

17 Here I will make a horn^a grow for David
        and set up a lamp for my anointed one.

18 I will clothe his enemies with shame,
        but the crown on his head will be resplendent."

Proverbs 12

1 Whoever loves discipline loves knowledge,
        but he who hates correction is stupid.

2 A good man obtains favor from the Lord,
        but the Lord condemns a crafty man.

3 A man cannot be established through wickedness,
        but the righteous cannot be uprooted.

4 A wife of noble character is her husband's crown,
        but a disgraceful wife is like decay in his bones.

5 The plans of the righteous are just,
        but the advice of the wicked is deceitful.

6 The words of the wicked lie in wait for blood,
        but the speech of the upright rescues them.

7 Wicked men are overthrown and are no more,
        but the house of the righteous stands firm.

8 A man is praised according to his wisdom,
        but men with warped minds are despised.

9 Better to be a nobody and yet have a servant
        than pretend to be somebody and have no food.

---

^a17 *Horn* here symbolizes strong one, that is, king.

10 A righteous man cares for the needs of his animal,
   but the kindest acts of the wicked are cruel.

11 He who works his land will have abundant food,
   but he who chases fantasies lacks judgment.

12 The wicked desire the plunder of evil men,
   but the root of the righteous flourishes.

13 An evil man is trapped by his sinful talk,
   but a righteous man escapes trouble.

14 From the fruit of his lips a man is filled with good
       things
   as surely as the work of his hands rewards him.

15 The way of a fool seems right to him,
   but a wise man listens to advice.

16 A fool shows his annoyance at once,
   but a prudent man overlooks an insult.

17 A truthful witness gives honest testimony,
   but a false witness tells lies.

18 Reckless words pierce like a sword,
   but the tongue of the wise brings healing.

19 Truthful lips endure forever,
   but a lying tongue lasts only a moment.

20 There is deceit in the hearts of those who plot evil,
   but joy for those who promote peace.

21 No harm befalls the righteous,
   but the wicked have their fill of trouble.

22 The Lord detests lying lips,
   but he delights in men who are truthful.

23 A prudent man keeps his knowledge to
        himself,
        but the heart of fools blurts out folly.

24 Diligent hands will rule,
        but laziness ends in slave labor.

25 An anxious heart weighs a man down,
        but a kind word cheers him up.

26 A righteous man is cautious in friendship, *a*
        but the way of the wicked leads them astray.

27 The lazy man does not roast *b* his game,
        but the diligent man prizes his possessions.

28 In the way of righteousness there is life;
        along that path is immortality.

DAY 13

Psalm 13
For the director of music. A psalm of David.

1 How long, O Lord? Will you forget me forever?
        How long will you hide your face from me?
2 How long must I wrestle with my thoughts
        and every day have sorrow in my heart?
        How long will my enemy triumph over me?
3 Look on me and answer, O Lord my God.
        Give light to my eyes, or I will sleep in death;
4 my enemy will say, "I have overcome him,"
        and my foes will rejoice when I fall.

*a*26 Or *man is a guide to his neighbor*   *b*27 The meaning of the
Hebrew for this word is uncertain.

5   But I trust in your unfailing love;
         my heart rejoices in your salvation.
6   I will sing to the Lord,
         for he has been good to me.

Psalm 43 [a]

1   Vindicate me, O God,
         and plead my cause against an
             ungodly nation;
         rescue me from deceitful
             and wicked men.
2   You are God my stronghold.
         Why have you rejected me?
     Why must I go about mourning,
         oppressed by the enemy?
3   Send forth your light and your truth,
         let them guide me;
     let them bring me to your holy mountain,
         to the place where you dwell.
4   Then will I go to the altar of God,
         to God, my joy and my delight.
     I will praise you with the harp,
         O God, my God.

5   Why are you downcast, O my soul?
         Why so disturbed within me?
     Put your hope in God,
         for I will yet praise him,
         my Savior and my God.

---

[a] In many Hebrew manuscripts Psalms 42 and 43 constitute one psalm.

Psalm 73
A psalm of Asaph.

1 Surely God is good to Israel,
   to those who are pure in heart.

2 But as for me, my feet had almost slipped;
   I had nearly lost my foothold.
3 For I envied the arrogant
   when I saw the prosperity of the wicked.

4 They have no struggles;
   their bodies are healthy and strong. *a*
5 They are free from the burdens common to man;
   they are not plagued by human ills.
6 Therefore pride is their necklace;
   they clothe themselves with violence.
7 From their callous hearts comes iniquity *b*;
   the evil conceits of their minds know
      no limits.
8 They scoff, and speak with malice;
   in their arrogance they threaten oppression.
9 Their mouths lay claim to heaven,
   and their tongues take possession of the earth.
10 Therefore their people turn to them
   and drink up waters in abundance. *c*
11 They say, "How can God know?
   Does the Most High have knowledge?"

12 This is what the wicked are like—
   always carefree, they increase in wealth.

a4 With a different word division of the Hebrew; Masoretic Text
struggles at their death; / their bodies are healthy *b7* Syriac (see also
Septuagint); Hebrew *Their eyes bulge with fat* *c10* The meaning of
the Hebrew for this verse is uncertain.

13 Surely in vain have I kept my heart pure;
     in vain have I washed my hands in
       innocence.
14 All day long I have been plagued;
     I have been punished every morning.

15 If I had said, "I will speak thus,"
     I would have betrayed your children.
16 When I tried to understand all this,
     it was oppressive to me
17 till I entered the sanctuary of God;
     then I understood their final destiny.

18 Surely you place them on slippery ground;
     you cast them down to ruin.
19 How suddenly are they destroyed,
     completely swept away by terrors!
20 As a dream when one awakes,
     so when you arise, O Lord,
       you will despise them as fantasies.

21 When my heart was grieved
     and my spirit embittered,
22 I was senseless and ignorant;
     I was a brute beast before you.

23 Yet I am always with you;
     you hold me by my right hand.
24 You guide me with your counsel,
     and afterward you will take me into glory.
25 Whom have I in heaven but you?
     And earth has nothing I desire besides you.
26 My flesh and my heart may fail,
     but God is the strength of my heart
       and my portion forever.

27 Those who are far from you will perish;
   you destroy all who are unfaithful to you.
28 But as for me, it is good to be near God.
   I have made the Sovereign Lord my refuge;
   I will tell of all your deeds.

Psalm 103
Of David.

1 Praise the Lord, O my soul;
   all my inmost being,
      praise his holy name.
2 Praise the Lord, O my soul,
   and forget not all his benefits—
3 who forgives all your sins
   and heals all your diseases,
4 who redeems your life from the pit
   and crowns you with love and compassion,
5 who satisfies your desires with good things
   so that your youth is renewed like the eagle's.

6 The Lord works righteousness
   and justice for all the oppressed.

7 He made known his ways to Moses,
   his deeds to the people of Israel:
8 The Lord is compassionate and gracious,
   slow to anger, abounding in love.
9 He will not always accuse,
   nor will he harbor his anger forever;
10 he does not treat us as our sins deserve
   or repay us according to our iniquities.
11 For as high as the heavens are above the earth,
   so great is his love for those who fear him;
12 as far as the east is from the west,

so far has he removed our transgressions from us.
13 As a father has compassion on his children,
   so the Lord has compassion on those who fear him;
14 for he knows how we are formed,
   he remembers that we are dust.
15 As for man, his days are like grass,
   he flourishes like a flower of the field;
16 the wind blows over it and it is gone,
   and its place remembers it no more.
17 But from everlasting to everlasting
   the Lord's love is with those who fear him,
   and his righteousness with their children's
      children—
18 with those who keep his covenant
   and remember to obey his precepts.

19 The Lord has established his throne in heaven,
   and his kingdom rules over all.

20 Praise the Lord, you his angels,
   you mighty ones who do his bidding,
   who obey his word.
21 Praise the Lord, all his heavenly hosts,
   you his servants who do his will.
22 Praise the Lord, all his works
   everywhere in his dominion.

   Praise the Lord, O my soul.

Psalm 133
A song of ascents. Of David.

1 How good and pleasant it is
   when brothers live together in unity!
2 It is like precious oil poured on the head,

running down on the beard,
running down on Aaron's beard,
down upon the collar of his robes.

3   It is as if the dew of Hermon
were falling on Mount Zion.
For there the Lord bestows his blessing,
even life forevermore.

Proverbs 13

1   A wise son heeds his father's instruction,
but a mocker does not listen to rebuke.

2   From the fruit of his lips a man enjoys good
things,
but the unfaithful have a craving for violence.

3   He who guards his lips guards his life,
but he who speaks rashly will come to ruin.

4   The sluggard craves and gets nothing,
but the desires of the diligent are fully satisfied.

5   The righteous hate what is false,
but the wicked bring shame and disgrace.

6   Righteousness guards the man of integrity,
but wickedness overthrows the sinner.

7   One man pretends to be rich, yet has nothing;
another pretends to be poor, yet has great
wealth.

8   A man's riches may ransom his life,
but a poor man hears no threat.

9   The light of the righteous shines brightly,
but the lamp of the wicked is snuffed out.

10 Pride only breeds quarrels,
      but wisdom is found in those who take advice.

11 Dishonest money dwindles away,
      but he who gathers money little by little makes
         it grow.

12 Hope deferred makes the heart sick,
      but a longing fulfilled is a tree of life.

13 He who scorns instruction will pay for it,
      but he who respects a command is rewarded.

14 The teaching of the wise is a fountain of life,
      turning a man from the snares of death.

15 Good understanding wins favor,
      but the way of the unfaithful is hard. [a]

16 Every prudent man acts out of knowledge,
      but a fool exposes his folly.

17 A wicked messenger falls into trouble,
      but a trustworthy envoy brings healing.

18 He who ignores discipline comes to poverty
         and shame,
      but whoever heeds correction is honored.

19 A longing fulfilled is sweet to the soul,
      but fools detest turning from evil.

20 He who walks with the wise grows wise,
      but a companion of fools suffers harm.

21 Misfortune pursues the sinner,
      but prosperity is the reward of the righteous.

[a]15 Or *unfaithful does not endure*

22 A good man leaves an inheritance for his
        children's children,
      but a sinner's wealth is stored up for the
        righteous.

23 A poor man's field may produce abundant
        food,
      but injustice sweeps it away.

24 He who spares the rod hates his son,
      but he who loves him is careful to discipline him.

25 The righteous eat to their hearts' content,
      but the stomach of the wicked goes hungry.

DAY 14

Psalm 14
For the director of music. Of David.

1 The fool *a* says in his heart,
        "There is no God."
      They are corrupt, their deeds are vile;
        there is no one who does good.

2 The Lord looks down from heaven
        on the sons of men
      to see if there are any who understand,
        any who seek God.

3 All have turned aside,
        they have together become corrupt;
      there is no one who does good,
        not even one.

a1 The Hebrew words rendered *fool* in Psalms denote one who is
morally deficient.

4   Will evildoers never learn—
         those who devour my people as men eat bread
         and who do not call on the Lord?
5   There they are, overwhelmed with dread,
         for God is present in the company of the righteous.
6   You evildoers frustrate the plans of the poor,
         but the Lord is their refuge.

7   Oh, that salvation for Israel would come out of Zion!
         When the Lord restores the fortunes of his
              people,
         let Jacob rejoice and Israel be glad!

Psalm 44

For the director of music. Of the Sons of Korah.
A *maskil.* [a]

1   We have heard with our ears, O God;
         our fathers have told us
     what you did in their days,
         in days long ago.
2   With your hand you drove out the nations
         and planted our fathers;
     you crushed the peoples
         and made our fathers flourish.
3   It was not by their sword that they won the land,
         nor did their arm bring them victory;
     it was your right hand, your arm,
         and the light of your face, for you loved them.

4   You are my King and my God,
         who decrees [b] victories for Jacob.

[a] Title: Probably a literary or musical term   [b] 4 Septuagint, Aquila
and Syriac; Hebrew *King, O God; / command*

5   Through you we push back our enemies;
      through your name we trample our foes.
6   I do not trust in my bow,
      my sword does not bring me victory;
7   but you give us victory over our enemies,
      you put our adversaries to shame.
8   In God we make our boast all day long,
      and we will praise your name forever.   *Selah*

9   But now you have rejected and humbled us;
      you no longer go out with our armies.
10   You made us retreat before the enemy,
      and our adversaries have plundered us.
11   You gave us up to be devoured like sheep
      and have scattered us among the nations.
12   You sold your people for a pittance,
      gaining nothing from their sale.

13   You have made us a reproach to our neighbors,
      the scorn and derision of those around us.
14   You have made us a byword among the nations;
      the peoples shake their heads at us.
15   My disgrace is before me all day long,
      and my face is covered with shame
16   at the taunts of those who reproach and revile me,
      because of the enemy, who is bent on revenge.

17   All this happened to us,
      though we had not forgotten you
      or been false to your covenant.
18   Our hearts had not turned back;
      our feet had not strayed from your path.
19   But you crushed us and made us a haunt for
        jackals
      and covered us over with deep darkness.

20 If we had forgotten the name of our God
or spread out our hands to a foreign god,
21 would not God have discovered it,
since he knows the secrets of the heart?
22 Yet for your sake we face death all day long;
we are considered as sheep to be slaughtered.

23 Awake, O Lord! Why do you sleep?
Rouse yourself! Do not reject us forever.
24 Why do you hide your face
and forget our misery and oppression?

25 We are brought down to the dust;
our bodies cling to the ground.
26 Rise up and help us;
redeem us because of your unfailing love.

Psalm 74
A *maskil* [a] of Asaph.

1 Why have you rejected us forever, O God?
Why does your anger smolder against the
sheep of your pasture?
2 Remember the people you purchased of old,
the tribe of your inheritance, whom you
redeemed—
Mount Zion, where you dwelt.
3 Turn your steps toward these everlasting ruins,
all this destruction the enemy has brought on
the sanctuary.

4 Your foes roared in the place where you met with us;
they set up their standards as signs.

---

[a] Title: Probably a literary or musical term

5   They behaved like men wielding axes
        to cut through a thicket of trees.
6   They smashed all the carved paneling
        with their axes and hatchets.
7   They burned your sanctuary to the ground;
        they defiled the dwelling place of your Name.
8   They said in their hearts, "We will crush them
        completely!"
    They burned every place where God was
        worshiped in the land.
9   We are given no miraculous signs;
        no prophets are left,
    and none of us knows how long this will be.

10 How long will the enemy mock you, O God?
        Will the foe revile your name forever?
11 Why do you hold back your hand, your right hand?
        Take it from the folds of your garment and
        destroy them!

12 But you, O God, are my king from of old;
        you bring salvation upon the earth.
13 It was you who split open the sea by your power;
        you broke the heads of the monster in the
        waters.
14 It was you who crushed the heads of Leviathan
        and gave him as food to the creatures of the
        desert.
15 It was you who opened up springs and streams;
        you dried up the ever flowing rivers.
16 The day is yours, and yours also the night;
        you established the sun and moon.
17 It was you who set all the boundaries of the earth;
        you made both summer and winter.

18 Remember how the enemy has mocked you, O Lord,
   how foolish people have reviled your name.
19 Do not hand over the life of your dove to wild
      beasts;
   do not forget the lives of your afflicted people
      forever.
20 Have regard for your covenant,
   because haunts of violence fill the dark places
      of the land.
21 Do not let the oppressed retreat in disgrace;
   may the poor and needy praise your name.

22 Rise up, O God, and defend your cause;
   remember how fools mock you all day long.
23 Do not ignore the clamor of your adversaries,
   the uproar of your enemies, which rises
      continually.

Psalm 104

1 Praise the Lord, O my soul.

   O Lord my God, you are very great;
   you are clothed with splendor and majesty.
2 He wraps himself in light as with a garment;
   he stretches out the heavens like a tent
3 and lays the beams of his upper chambers
      on their waters.
   He makes the clouds his chariot
   and rides on the wings of the wind.
4 He makes winds his messengers, *a*
   flames of fire his servants.

*a*4 Or *angels*

5   He set the earth on its foundations;
        it can never be moved.
6   You covered it with the deep as with a garment;
        the waters stood above the mountains.
7   But at your rebuke the waters fled,
        at the sound of your thunder they took to flight;
8   they flowed over the mountains,
        they went down into the valleys,
        to the place you assigned for them.
9   You set a boundary they cannot cross;
        never again will they cover the earth.

10 He makes springs pour water into the ravines;
        it flows between the mountains.
11 They give water to all the beasts of the field;
        the wild donkeys quench their thirst.
12 The birds of the air nest by the waters;
        they sing among the branches.
13 He waters the mountains from his upper chambers;
        the earth is satisfied by the fruit of his work.
14 He makes grass grow for the cattle,
        and plants for man to cultivate—
        bringing forth food from the earth:
15 wine that gladdens the heart of man,
        oil to make his face shine,
        and bread that sustains his heart.
16 The trees of the Lord are well watered,
        the cedars of Lebanon that he planted.
17 There the birds make their nests;
        the stork has its home in the pine trees.
18 The high mountains belong to the wild goats;
        the crags are a refuge for the coneys. [a]

[a] 18 That is, the hyrax or rock badger

19 The moon marks off the seasons,
  and the sun knows when to go down.
20 You bring darkness, it becomes night,
  and all the beasts of the forest prowl.
21 The lions roar for their prey
  and seek their food from God.
22 The sun rises, and they steal away;
  they return and lie down in their dens.
23 Then man goes out to his work,
  to his labor until evening.

24 How many are your works, O Lord!
  In wisdom you made them all;
  the earth is full of your creatures.
25 There is the sea, vast and spacious,
  teeming with creatures beyond number—
  living things both large and small.
26 There the ships go to and fro,
  and the leviathan, which you formed to frolic
    there.

27 These all look to you
  to give them their food at the proper time.
28 When you give it to them,
  they gather it up;
when you open your hand,
  they are satisfied with good things.
29 When you hide your face,
  they are terrified;
when you take away their breath,
  they die and return to the dust.
30 When you send your Spirit,
  they are created,
  and you renew the face of the earth.

31 May the glory of the Lord endure forever;
     may the Lord rejoice in his works—
32 he who looks at the earth, and it trembles,
     who touches the mountains, and they smoke.

33 I will sing to the Lord all my life;
     I will sing praise to my God as long
       as I live.
34 May my meditation be pleasing to him,
     as I rejoice in the Lord.
35 But may sinners vanish from the earth
     and the wicked be no more.

Praise the Lord, O my soul.

Praise the Lord. *a*

Psalm 134

A song of ascents.

1 Praise the Lord, all you servants of the Lord
     who minister by night in the house of the Lord.
2 Lift up your hands in the sanctuary
     and praise the Lord.
3 May the Lord, the Maker of heaven and earth,
     bless you from Zion.

Proverbs 14

1 The wise woman builds her house,
     but with her own hands the foolish
      one tears hers down.

*a*35 Hebrew *Hallelu Yah*; in the Septuagint this line stands at the
beginning of Psalm 105.

DAY 14

2   He whose walk is upright fears the Lord,
       but he whose ways are devious despises him.

3   A fool's talk brings a rod to his back,
       but the lips of the wise protect them.

4   Where there are no oxen, the manger is empty,
       but from the strength of an ox comes an
          abundant harvest.

5   A truthful witness does not deceive,
       but a false witness pours out lies.

6   The mocker seeks wisdom and finds none,
       but knowledge comes easily to the discerning.

7   Stay away from a foolish man,
       for you will not find knowledge on his lips.

8   The wisdom of the prudent is to give thought to
          their ways,
       but the folly of fools is deception.

9   Fools mock at making amends for sin,
       but goodwill is found among the upright.

10 Each heart knows its own bitterness,
       and no one else can share its joy.

11 The house of the wicked will be destroyed,
       but the tent of the upright will flourish.

12 There is a way that seems right to a man,
       but in the end it leads to death.

13 Even in laughter the heart may ache,
       and joy may end in grief.

14 The faithless will be fully repaid for their ways,
       and the good man rewarded for his.

15 A simple man believes anything,
   but a prudent man gives thought to his steps.

16 A wise man fears the Lord and shuns evil,
   but a fool is hotheaded and reckless.

17 A quick-tempered man does foolish things,
   and a crafty man is hated.

18 The simple inherit folly,
   but the prudent are crowned with knowledge.

19 Evil men will bow down in the presence of the
   good,
   and the wicked at the gates of the righteous.

20 The poor are shunned even by their neighbors,
   but the rich have many friends.

21 He who despises his neighbor sins,
   but blessed is he who is kind to the needy.

22 Do not those who plot evil go astray?
   But those who plan what is good find *a* love
   and faithfulness.

23 All hard work brings a profit,
   but mere talk leads only to poverty.

24 The wealth of the wise is their crown,
   but the folly of fools yields folly.

25 A truthful witness saves lives,
   but a false witness is deceitful.

26 He who fears the Lord has a secure fortress,
   and for his children it will be a refuge.

*a*22 Or *show*

27 The fear of the Lord is a fountain of life,
     turning a man from the snares of death.

28 A large population is a king's glory,
     but without subjects a prince is ruined.

29 A patient man has great understanding,
     but a quick-tempered man displays folly.

30 A heart at peace gives life to the body,
     but envy rots the bones.

31 He who oppresses the poor shows contempt for
        their Maker,
     but whoever is kind to the needy honors God.

32 When calamity comes, the wicked are brought down,
     but even in death the righteous have a refuge.

33 Wisdom reposes in the heart of the discerning
     and even among fools she lets herself be known. *a*

34 Righteousness exalts a nation,
     but sin is a disgrace to any people.

35 A king delights in a wise servant,
     but a shameful servant incurs his wrath.

DAY 15

Psalm 15
A psalm of David.

1 Lord, who may dwell in your sanctuary?
     Who may live on your holy hill?

a33 Hebrew; Septuagint and Syriac / *but in the heart of fools she is not known*

2 He whose walk is blameless
    and who does what is righteous,
  who speaks the truth from his heart
3   and has no slander on his tongue,
  who does his neighbor no wrong
    and casts no slur on his fellow man,
4 who despises a vile man
    but honors those who fear the Lord,
  who keeps his oath
    even when it hurts,
5 who lends his money without usury
    and does not accept a bribe against the innocent.

  He who does these things
    will never be shaken.

Psalm 45

For the director of music. To the tune of "Lilies."
Of the Sons of Korah. A *maskil.* [a] A wedding song.

1 My heart is stirred by a noble theme
    as I recite my verses for the king;
  my tongue is the pen of a skillful writer.

2 You are the most excellent of men
    and your lips have been anointed with grace,
  since God has blessed you forever.

3 Gird your sword upon your side, O mighty one;
    clothe yourself with splendor and majesty.

4 In your majesty ride forth victoriously
    in behalf of truth, humility and righteousness;
  let your right hand display awesome deeds.

---

[a] Title: Probably a literary or musical term

5   Let your sharp arrows pierce the hearts of the
        king's enemies;
      let the nations fall beneath your feet.

6   Your throne, O God, will last for ever and ever;
      a scepter of justice will be the scepter of your
        kingdom.

7   You love righteousness and hate wickedness;
      therefore God, your God, has set you above
        your companions
      by anointing you with the oil of joy.

8   All your robes are fragrant with myrrh and aloes
        and cassia;
      from palaces adorned with ivory
      the music of the strings makes you glad.

9   Daughters of kings are among your honored
        women;
      at your right hand is the royal bride in gold of
        Ophir.

10 Listen, O daughter, consider and give ear:
      Forget your people and your father's house.

11 The king is enthralled by your beauty;
      honor him, for he is your lord.

12 The Daughter of Tyre will come with a gift, [a]
      men of wealth will seek your favor.

13 All glorious is the princess within her chamber;
      her gown is interwoven with gold.

14 In embroidered garments she is led to the king;
      her virgin companions follow her
      and are brought to you.

15 They are led in with joy and gladness;
      they enter the palace of the king.

[a]12 Or *A Tyrian robe is among the gifts*

16 Your sons will take the place of your fathers;
  you will make them princes throughout the land.
17 I will perpetuate your memory through all
    generations;
  therefore the nations will praise you for ever
    and ever.

Psalm 75
For the director of music. To the tune of
"Do Not Destroy." A psalm of Asaph. A song.

1 We give thanks to you, O God,
  we give thanks, for your Name is near;
  men tell of your wonderful deeds.

2 You say, "I choose the appointed time;
  it is I who judge uprightly.
3 When the earth and all its people quake,
  it is I who hold its pillars firm.   *Selah*
4 To the arrogant I say, 'Boast no more,'
  and to the wicked, 'Do not lift up your horns.
5 Do not lift your horns against heaven;
  do not speak with outstretched neck.'"

6 No one from the east or the west
  or from the desert can exalt a man.
7 But it is God who judges:
  He brings one down, he exalts another.
8 In the hand of the Lord is a cup
  full of foaming wine mixed with spices;
  he pours it out, and all the wicked of the earth
    drink it down to its very dregs.

9 As for me, I will declare this forever;
  I will sing praise to the God of Jacob.

10 I will cut off the horns of all the wicked,
       but the horns of the righteous will be lifted up.

Psalm 105

1 Give thanks to the Lord, call on his name;
       make known among the nations what he has
          done.
2 Sing to him, sing praise to him;
       tell of all his wonderful acts.
3 Glory in his holy name;
       let the hearts of those who seek the Lord rejoice.
4 Look to the Lord and his strength;
       seek his face always.

5 Remember the wonders he has done,
       his miracles, and the judgments he
          pronounced,
6 O descendants of Abraham his servant,
       O sons of Jacob, his chosen ones.
7 He is the Lord our God;
       his judgments are in all the earth.

8 He remembers his covenant forever,
       the word he commanded, for a thousand
          generations,
9 the covenant he made with Abraham,
       the oath he swore to Isaac.
10 He confirmed it to Jacob as a decree,
       to Israel as an everlasting covenant:
11 "To you I will give the land of Canaan
       as the portion you will inherit."

12 When they were but few in number,
       few indeed, and strangers in it,

13 they wandered from nation to nation,
    from one kingdom to another.
14 He allowed no one to oppress them;
    for their sake he rebuked kings:
15 "Do not touch my anointed ones;
    do my prophets no harm."

16 He called down famine on the land
    and destroyed all their supplies of food;
17 and he sent a man before them—
    Joseph, sold as a slave.
18 They bruised his feet with shackles,
    his neck was put in irons,
19 till what he foretold came to pass,
    till the word of the Lord proved him true.
20 The king sent and released him,
    the ruler of peoples set him free.
21 He made him master of his household,
    ruler over all he possessed,
22 to instruct his princes as he pleased
    and teach his elders wisdom.

23 Then Israel entered Egypt;
    Jacob lived as an alien in the land of Ham.
24 The Lord made his people very fruitful;
    he made them too numerous for their foes,
25 whose hearts he turned to hate his people,
    to conspire against his servants.
26 He sent Moses his servant,
    and Aaron, whom he had chosen.
27 They performed his miraculous signs among
    them,
    his wonders in the land of Ham.
28 He sent darkness and made the land dark—
    for had they not rebelled against his words?

29 He turned their waters into blood,
   causing their fish to die.
30 Their land teemed with frogs,
   which went up into the bedrooms of their rulers.
31 He spoke, and there came swarms of flies,
   and gnats throughout their country.
32 He turned their rain into hail,
   with lightning throughout their land;
33 he struck down their vines and fig trees
   and shattered the trees of their country.
34 He spoke, and the locusts came,
   grasshoppers without number;
35 they ate up every green thing in their land,
   ate up the produce of their soil.
36 Then he struck down all the firstborn in their land,
   the firstfruits of all their manhood.

37 He brought out Israel, laden with silver and gold,
   and from among their tribes no one faltered.
38 Egypt was glad when they left,
   because dread of Israel had fallen on them.
39 He spread out a cloud as a covering,
   and a fire to give light at night.
40 They asked, and he brought them quail
   and satisfied them with the bread of heaven.
41 He opened the rock, and water gushed out;
   like a river it flowed in the desert.

42 For he remembered his holy promise
   given to his servant Abraham.
43 He brought out his people with rejoicing,
   his chosen ones with shouts of joy;
44 he gave them the lands of the nations,
   and they fell heir to what others had
       toiled for—

45   that they might keep his precepts
        and observe his laws.

Praise the Lord. [a]

Psalm 135

1   Praise the Lord. [b]

Praise the name of the Lord;
        praise him, you servants of the Lord,
2   you who minister in the house of the Lord,
        in the courts of the house of our God.

3   Praise the Lord, for the Lord is good;
        sing praise to his name, for that is pleasant.
4   For the Lord has chosen Jacob to be his own,
        Israel to be his treasured possession.

5   I know that the Lord is great,
        that our Lord is greater than all gods.
6   The Lord does whatever pleases him,
        in the heavens and on the earth,
        in the seas and all their depths.
7   He makes clouds rise from the ends of the earth;
        he sends lightning with the rain
        and brings out the wind from his storehouses.

8   He struck down the firstborn of Egypt,
        the firstborn of men and animals.
9   He sent his signs and wonders into your midst,
            O Egypt,
        against Pharaoh and all his servants.
10 He struck down many nations

---

[a]45 Hebrew *Hallelu Yah*   [b]1 Hebrew *Hallelu Yah*; also in verses 3 and 21

and killed mighty kings—
11 Sihon king of the Amorites,
Og king of Bashan
and all the kings of Canaan—
12 and he gave their land as an inheritance,
an inheritance to his people Israel.

13 Your name, O Lord, endures forever,
your renown, O Lord, through all generations.
14 For the Lord will vindicate his people
and have compassion on his servants.

15 The idols of the nations are silver and gold,
made by the hands of men.
16 They have mouths, but cannot speak,
eyes, but they cannot see;
17 they have ears, but cannot hear,
nor is there breath in their mouths.
18 Those who make them will be like them,
and so will all who trust in them.

19 O house of Israel, praise the Lord;
O house of Aaron, praise the Lord;
20 O house of Levi, praise the Lord;
you who fear him, praise the Lord.
21 Praise be to the Lord from Zion,
to him who dwells in Jerusalem.

Praise the Lord.

Proverbs 15

1 A gentle answer turns away wrath,
but a harsh word stirs up anger.

2 The tongue of the wise commends knowledge,

but the mouth of the fool gushes folly.

3   The eyes of the Lord are everywhere,
       keeping watch on the wicked and the good.

4   The tongue that brings healing is a tree of life,
       but a deceitful tongue crushes the spirit.

5   A fool spurns his father's discipline,
       but whoever heeds correction shows
           prudence.

6   The house of the righteous contains great
           treasure,
       but the income of the wicked brings them
           trouble.

7   The lips of the wise spread knowledge;
       not so the hearts of fools.

8   The Lord detests the sacrifice of the wicked,
       but the prayer of the upright pleases him.

9   The Lord detests the way of the wicked
       but he loves those who pursue righteousness.

10 Stern discipline awaits him who leaves the path;
       he who hates correction will die.

11 Death and Destruction [a] lie open before the Lord—
       how much more the hearts of men!

12 A mocker resents correction;
       he will not consult the wise.

13 A happy heart makes the face cheerful,
       but heartache crushes the spirit.

[a]11 Hebrew *Sheol and Abaddon*

14 The discerning heart seeks knowledge,
   but the mouth of a fool feeds on folly.

15 All the days of the oppressed are wretched,
   but the cheerful heart has a continual feast.

16 Better a little with the fear of the Lord
   than great wealth with turmoil.

17 Better a meal of vegetables where there is love
   than a fattened calf with hatred.

18 A hot-tempered man stirs up dissension,
   but a patient man calms a quarrel.

19 The way of the sluggard is blocked with thorns,
   but the path of the upright is a highway.

20 A wise son brings joy to his father,
   but a foolish man despises his mother.

21 Folly delights a man who lacks judgment,
   but a man of understanding keeps a straight
      course.

22 Plans fail for lack of counsel,
   but with many advisers they succeed.

23 A man finds joy in giving an apt reply—
   and how good is a timely word!

24 The path of life leads upward for the wise
   to keep him from going down to the grave. *a*

25 The Lord tears down the proud man's house
   but he keeps the widow's boundaries intact.

---

*a*24 Hebrew *Sheol*

26 The Lord detests the thoughts of the wicked,
    but those of the pure are pleasing to him.

27 A greedy man brings trouble to his family,
    but he who hates bribes will live.

28 The heart of the righteous weighs its answers,
    but the mouth of the wicked gushes evil.

29 The Lord is far from the wicked
    but he hears the prayer of the righteous.

30 A cheerful look brings joy to the heart,
    and good news gives health to the bones.

31 He who listens to a life-giving rebuke
    will be at home among the wise.

32 He who ignores discipline despises himself,
    but whoever heeds correction gains
       understanding.

33 The fear of the Lord teaches a man wisdom, *a*
    and humility comes before honor.

DAY 16

Psalm 16
A *miktam* *b* of David.

1 Keep me safe, O God,
    for in you I take refuge.

2 I said to the Lord, "You are my Lord;
    apart from you I have no good thing."

*a*33 Or *Wisdom teaches the fear of the Lord*   *b* Title: Probably a literary
or musical term

3   As for the saints who are in the land,
        they are the glorious ones in whom is all my
            delight. [a]

4   The sorrows of those will increase
        who run after other gods.
    I will not pour out their libations of blood
        or take up their names on my lips.

5   Lord, you have assigned me my portion
            and my cup;
        you have made my lot secure.

6   The boundary lines have fallen for me in
            pleasant places;
        surely I have a delightful inheritance.

7   I will praise the Lord, who counsels me;
        even at night my heart instructs me.

8   I have set the Lord always before me.
        Because he is at my right hand,
        I will not be shaken.

9   Therefore my heart is glad and my tongue
            rejoices;
        my body also will rest secure,

10 because you will not abandon me to the grave, [b]
        nor will you let your Holy One [c] see decay.

11 You have made [d] known to me the path of life;
        you will fill me with joy in your presence,
        with eternal pleasures at your right hand.

[a]3 Or As for the pagan priests who are in the land / and the nobles in whom
all delight, I said: [b]10 Hebrew Sheol   [c]10 Or your faithful one
[d]11 Or You will make

Psalm 46

For the director of music. Of the Sons of Korah.
According to *alamoth*. *^a* A song.

1   God is our refuge and strength,
      an ever-present help in trouble.
2   Therefore we will not fear, though the earth give
         way
      and the mountains fall into the heart of the sea,
3   though its waters roar and foam
      and the mountains quake with their
         surging.   *Selah*

4   There is a river whose streams make glad the city
         of God,
      the holy place where the Most High dwells.
5   God is within her, she will not fall;
      God will help her at break of day.
6   Nations are in uproar, kingdoms fall;
      he lifts his voice, the earth melts.
7   The Lord Almighty is with us;
      the God of Jacob is our fortress.   *Selah*

8   Come and see the works of the Lord,
      the desolations he has brought on the earth.
9   He makes wars cease to the ends of the earth;
      he breaks the bow and shatters the spear,
      he burns the shields *^b* with fire.
10   "Be still, and know that I am God;
      I will be exalted among the nations,
      I will be exalted in the earth."

11   The Lord Almighty is with us;
      the God of Jacob is our fortress.   *Selah*

^a Title: Probably a musical term   *^b9* Or *chariots*

Psalm 76

For the director of music. With stringed instruments.
A psalm of Asaph. A song.

1 In Judah God is known;
      his name is great in Israel.
2 His tent is in Salem,
      his dwelling place in Zion.
3 There he broke the flashing arrows,
      the shields and the swords, the weapons
         of war.   *Selah*

4 You are resplendent with light,
      more majestic than mountains rich
         with game.
5 Valiant men lie plundered,
      they sleep their last sleep;
   not one of the warriors
      can lift his hands.
6 At your rebuke, O God of Jacob,
      both horse and chariot lie still.

7 You alone are to be feared.
      Who can stand before you when you
         are angry?
8 From heaven you pronounced judgment,
      and the land feared and was quiet—
9 when you, O God, rose up to judge,
      to save all the afflicted of the land.   *Selah*
10 Surely your wrath against men brings
         you praise,
      and the survivors of your wrath are
         restrained. [a]

*a10 Or Surely the wrath of men brings you praise, / and with the remainder
of wrath you arm yourself*

11 Make vows to the Lord your God and
            fulfill them;
        let all the neighboring lands
        bring gifts to the One to be feared.
12 He breaks the spirit of rulers;
        he is feared by the kings of the earth.

Psalm 106

1 Praise the Lord. *a*

    Give thanks to the Lord, for he is good;
        his love endures forever.
2 Who can proclaim the mighty acts of the Lord
        or fully declare his praise?
3 Blessed are they who maintain justice,
        who constantly do what is right.
4 Remember me, O Lord, when you show favor
            to your people,
        come to my aid when you save them,
5 that I may enjoy the prosperity of your chosen
            ones,
        that I may share in the joy of your nation
        and join your inheritance in giving praise.

6 We have sinned, even as our fathers did;
        we have done wrong and acted wickedly.
7 When our fathers were in Egypt,
        they gave no thought to your miracles;
        they did not remember your many kindnesses,
        and they rebelled by the sea, the Red Sea. *b*
8 Yet he saved them for his name's sake,

---

*a*1 Hebrew *Hallelu Yah*; also in verse 48   *b*7 Hebrew *Yam Suph*; that
is, Sea of Reeds; also in verses 9 and 22

to make his mighty power known.
9 He rebuked the Red Sea, and it dried up;
     he led them through the depths as through a
          desert.
10 He saved them from the hand of the foe;
     from the hand of the enemy he redeemed
          them.
11 The waters covered their adversaries;
     not one of them survived.
12 Then they believed his promises
     and sang his praise.

13 But they soon forgot what he had done
     and did not wait for his counsel.
14 In the desert they gave in to their craving;
     in the wasteland they put God to the test.
15 So he gave them what they asked for,
     but sent a wasting disease upon them.

16 In the camp they grew envious of Moses
     and of Aaron, who was consecrated to
          the Lord.
17 The earth opened up and swallowed Dathan;
     it buried the company of Abiram.
18 Fire blazed among their followers;
     a flame consumed the wicked.

19 At Horeb they made a calf
     and worshiped an idol cast from metal.
20 They exchanged their Glory
     for an image of a bull, which eats grass.
21 They forgot the God who saved them,
     who had done great things in Egypt,
22 miracles in the land of Ham
     and awesome deeds by the Red Sea.

23 So he said he would destroy them—
  had not Moses, his chosen one,
 stood in the breach before him
  to keep his wrath from destroying them.

24 Then they despised the pleasant land;
  they did not believe his promise.
25 They grumbled in their tents
  and did not obey the Lord.
26 So he swore to them with uplifted hand
  that he would make them fall in the desert,
27 make their descendants fall among the nations
  and scatter them throughout the lands.

28 They yoked themselves to the Baal of Peor
  and ate sacrifices offered to lifeless gods;
29 they provoked the Lord to anger by their
    wicked deeds,
  and a plague broke out among them.
30 But Phinehas stood up and intervened,
  and the plague was checked.
31 This was credited to him as righteousness
  for endless generations to come.

32 By the waters of Meribah they angered
    the Lord,
  and trouble came to Moses because
    of them;
33 for they rebelled against the Spirit of God,
  and rash words came from Moses' lips. *a*

34 They did not destroy the peoples
  as the Lord had commanded them,
35 but they mingled with the nations

a33 Or against his spirit, / and rash words came from his lips and adopted their customs.

36 They worshiped their idols,
which became a snare to them.

37 They sacrificed their sons
and their daughters to demons.

38 They shed innocent blood,
the blood of their sons and daughters,
whom they sacrificed to the idols of Canaan,
and the land was desecrated by their blood.

39 They defiled themselves by what they did;
by their deeds they prostituted themselves.

40 Therefore the Lord was angry with
his people
and abhorred his inheritance.

41 He handed them over to the nations,
and their foes ruled over them.

42 Their enemies oppressed them
and subjected them to their power.

43 Many times he delivered them,
but they were bent on rebellion
and they wasted away in their sin.

44 But he took note of their distress
when he heard their cry;

45 for their sake he remembered his covenant
and out of his great love he relented.

46 He caused them to be pitied
by all who held them captive.

47 Save us, O Lord our God,
and gather us from the nations,
that we may give thanks to your
holy name
and glory in your praise.

48 Praise be to the Lord, the God of Israel,
    from everlasting to everlasting.
  Let all the people say, "Amen!"

  Praise the Lord.

Psalm 136

1 Give thanks to the Lord, for he is good.
    His love endures forever.

2 Give thanks to the God of gods.
    His love endures forever.

3 Give thanks to the Lord of lords:
    His love endures forever.

4 to him who alone does great wonders,
    His love endures forever.

5 who by his understanding made the heavens,
    His love endures forever.

6 who spread out the earth upon the waters,
    His love endures forever.

7 who made the great lights—
    His love endures forever.

8 the sun to govern the day,
    His love endures forever.

9 the moon and stars to govern the night;
    His love endures forever.

10 to him who struck down the firstborn of Egypt
    His love endures forever.

11 and brought Israel out from among them
His love endures forever.

12 with a mighty hand and outstretched arm;
His love endures forever.

13 to him who divided the Red Sea *a* asunder
His love endures forever.

14 and brought Israel through the midst of it,
His love endures forever.

15 but swept Pharaoh and his army into the Red Sea;
His love endures forever.

16 to him who led his people through the desert,
His love endures forever.

17 who struck down great kings,
His love endures forever.

18 and killed mighty kings—
His love endures forever.

19 Sihon king of the Amorites
His love endures forever.

20 and Og king of Bashan—
His love endures forever.

21 and gave their land as an inheritance,
His love endures forever.

22 an inheritance to his servant Israel;
His love endures forever.

23 to the One who remembered us in our low estate
His love endures forever.

*a*13 Hebrew *Yam Suph;* that is, Sea of Reeds; also in verse 15

24 and freed us from our enemies,
                    His love endures forever.

25 and who gives food to every creature.
                    His love endures forever.

26 Give thanks to the God of heaven.
                    His love endures forever.

Proverbs 16

1   To man belong the plans of the heart,
      but from the Lord comes the reply of the tongue.

2   All a man's ways seem innocent to him,
      but motives are weighed by the Lord.

3   Commit to the Lord whatever you do,
      and your plans will succeed.

4   The Lord works out everything for his own
            ends—
      even the wicked for a day of disaster.

5   The Lord detests all the proud of heart.
      Be sure of this: They will not go unpunished.

6   Through love and faithfulness sin is atoned for;
      through the fear of the Lord a man avoids evil.

7   When a man's ways are pleasing to the Lord,
      he makes even his enemies live at peace with
            him.

8   Better a little with righteousness
      than much gain with injustice.

9   In his heart a man plans his course,
      but the Lord determines his steps.

10 The lips of a king speak as an oracle,
   and his mouth should not betray justice.

11 Honest scales and balances are from the Lord;
   all the weights in the bag are of his making.

12 Kings detest wrongdoing,
   for a throne is established through
       righteousness.

13 Kings take pleasure in honest lips;
   they value a man who speaks the truth.

14 A king's wrath is a messenger of death,
   but a wise man will appease it.

15 When a king's face brightens, it means life;
   his favor is like a rain cloud in spring.

16 How much better to get wisdom than gold,
   to choose understanding rather than silver!

17 The highway of the upright avoids evil;
   he who guards his way guards his life.

18 Pride goes before destruction,
   a haughty spirit before a fall.

19 Better to be lowly in spirit and among
       the oppressed
   than to share plunder with the proud.

20 Whoever gives heed to instruction prospers,
   and blessed is he who trusts in the Lord.

21 The wise in heart are called discerning,
   and pleasant words promote instruction. [a]

---

[a]21 Or *words make a man persuasive*

22 Understanding is a fountain of life to those who
    have it,
      but folly brings punishment to fools.

23 A wise man's heart guides his mouth,
    and his lips promote instruction. [a]

24 Pleasant words are a honeycomb,
    sweet to the soul and healing to the bones.

25 There is a way that seems right to a man,
    but in the end it leads to death.

26 The laborer's appetite works for him;
    his hunger drives him on.

27 A scoundrel plots evil,
    and his speech is like a scorching fire.

28 A perverse man stirs up dissension,
    and a gossip separates close friends.

29 A violent man entices his neighbor
    and leads him down a path that is not good.

30 He who winks with his eye is plotting perversity;
    he who purses his lips is bent on evil.

31 Gray hair is a crown of splendor;
    it is attained by a righteous life.

32 Better a patient man than a warrior,
    a man who controls his temper than
      one who takes a city.

33 The lot is cast into the lap,
    but its every decision is from the Lord.

[a]23 Or *mouth / and makes his lips persuasive*

DAY 17

Psalms 17
A prayer of David.

1   Hear, O Lord, my righteous plea;
       listen to my cry.
    Give ear to my prayer—
       it does not rise from deceitful lips.
2   May my vindication come from you;
       may your eyes see what is right.

3   Though you probe my heart and examine
          me at night,
       though you test me, you will find nothing;
       I have resolved that my mouth will not sin.
4   As for the deeds of men—
       by the word of your lips
    I have kept myself
       from the ways of the violent.
5   My steps have held to your paths;
       my feet have not slipped.
6   I call on you, O God, for you will answer me;
       give ear to me and hear my prayer.
7   Show the wonder of your great love,
       you who save by your right hand
       those who take refuge in you from their foes.
8   Keep me as the apple of your eye;
       hide me in the shadow of your wings
9   from the wicked who assail me,
       from my mortal enemies who surround me.

10   They close up their callous hearts,
        and their mouths speak with arrogance.
11   They have tracked me down, they now surround me,

      with eyes alert, to throw me to the ground.
12 They are like a lion hungry for prey,
      like a great lion crouching in cover.

13 Rise up, O Lord, confront them, bring them down;
      rescue me from the wicked by your sword.
14 O Lord, by your hand save me from such men,
      from men of this world whose reward is in this
         life.

      You still the hunger of those you cherish;
      their sons have plenty,
      and they store up wealth for their children.
15 And I—in righteousness I will see your face;
      when I awake, I will be satisfied with seeing
        your likeness.

Psalm 47

For the director of music. Of the Sons of Korah.
A psalm.

1 Clap your hands, all you nations;
      shout to God with cries of joy.
2 How awesome is the Lord Most High,
      the great King over all the earth!
3 He subdued nations under us,
      peoples under our feet.
4 He chose our inheritance for us,
      the pride of Jacob, whom he loved.   *Selah*

5 God has ascended amid shouts of joy,
      the Lord amid the sounding of trumpets.
6 Sing praises to God, sing praises;
      sing praises to our King, sing praises.

7 For God is the King of all the earth;

sing to him a psalm *a* of praise.
8 God reigns over the nations;
God is seated on his holy throne.
9 The nobles of the nations assemble
as the people of the God of Abraham,
for the kings *b* of the earth belong to God;
he is greatly exalted.

Psalm 77

For the director of music. For Jeduthun.
Of Asaph. A psalm.

1 I cried out to God for help;
I cried out to God to hear me.
2 When I was in distress, I sought the Lord;
at night I stretched out untiring hands
and my soul refused to be comforted.

3 I remembered you, O God, and I groaned;
I mused, and my spirit grew faint.   *Selah*
4 You kept my eyes from closing;
I was too troubled to speak.
5 I thought about the former days,
the years of long ago;
6 I remembered my songs in the night.
My heart mused and my spirit inquired:

7 "Will the Lord reject forever?
Will he never show his favor again?
8 Has his unfailing love vanished forever?
Has his promise failed for all time?
9 Has God forgotten to be merciful?

---

*a*7 Or *a maskil* (probably a literary or musical term)   *b*9 Or *shields*

Has he in anger withheld his
   compassion?"   *Selah*

10 Then I thought, "To this I will appeal:
       the years of the right hand of the Most High."
11 I will remember the deeds of the Lord;
       yes, I will remember your miracles of long ago.
12 I will meditate on all your works
       and consider all your mighty deeds.

13 Your ways, O God, are holy.
       What god is so great as our God?
14 You are the God who performs miracles;
       you display your power among the peoples.
15 With your mighty arm you redeemed your
           people,
       the descendants of Jacob and Joseph.   *Selah*

16 The waters saw you, O God,
       the waters saw you and writhed;
       the very depths were convulsed.
17 The clouds poured down water,
       the skies resounded with thunder;
       your arrows flashed back and forth.
18 Your thunder was heard in the whirlwind,
       your lightning lit up the world;
       the earth trembled and quaked.
19 Your path led through the sea,
       your way through the mighty waters,
       though your footprints were not seen.

20 You led your people like a flock
       by the hand of Moses and Aaron.

Psalm 107

1   Give thanks to the Lord, for he is good;
     his love endures forever.
2   Let the redeemed of the Lord say this—
     those he redeemed from the hand of the foe,
3   those he gathered from the lands,
     from east and west, from north and south. *a*

4   Some wandered in desert wastelands,
     finding no way to a city where they could settle.
5   They were hungry and thirsty,
     and their lives ebbed away.
6   Then they cried out to the Lord in their trouble,
     and he delivered them from their distress.
7   He led them by a straight way
     to a city where they could settle.
8   Let them give thanks to the Lord for his
       unfailing love
     and his wonderful deeds for men,
9   for he satisfies the thirsty
     and fills the hungry with good things.

10   Some sat in darkness and the deepest gloom,
     prisoners suffering in iron chains,
11   for they had rebelled against the words of God
     and despised the counsel of the Most High.
12   So he subjected them to bitter labor;
     they stumbled, and there was no one to help.
13   Then they cried to the Lord in their trouble,
     and he saved them from their distress.
14   He brought them out of darkness and the
       deepest gloom

a3 Hebrew north and the sea

and broke away their chains.

15 Let them give thanks to the Lord for his unfailing
    love
    and his wonderful deeds for men,
16 for he breaks down gates of bronze
    and cuts through bars of iron.

17 Some became fools through their rebellious ways
    and suffered affliction because of their
    iniquities.
18 They loathed all food
    and drew near the gates of death.
19 Then they cried to the Lord in their trouble,
    and he saved them from their distress.
20 He sent forth his word and healed them;
    he rescued them from the grave.
21 Let them give thanks to the Lord for his unfailing
    love
    and his wonderful deeds for men.
22 Let them sacrifice thank offerings
    and tell of his works with songs of joy.

23 Others went out on the sea in ships;
    they were merchants on the mighty waters.
24 They saw the works of the Lord,
    his wonderful deeds in the deep.
25 For he spoke and stirred up a tempest
    that lifted high the waves.
26 They mounted up to the heavens and went down
    to the depths;
    in their peril their courage melted away.
27 They reeled and staggered like drunken men;
    they were at their wits' end.
28 Then they cried out to the Lord in their trouble,
    and he brought them out of their distress.

29 He stilled the storm to a whisper;
   the waves of the sea were hushed.
30 They were glad when it grew calm,
   and he guided them to their desired haven.
31 Let them give thanks to the Lord for his unfailing love
   and his wonderful deeds for men.
32 Let them exalt him in the assembly of the people
   and praise him in the council of the elders.

33 He turned rivers into a desert,
   flowing springs into thirsty ground,
34 and fruitful land into a salt waste,
   because of the wickedness of those who lived there.
35 He turned the desert into pools of water
   and the parched ground into flowing springs;
36 there he brought the hungry to live,
   and they founded a city where they could settle.
37 They sowed fields and planted vineyards
   that yielded a fruitful harvest;
38 he blessed them, and their numbers greatly
      increased,
   and he did not let their herds diminish.

39 Then their numbers decreased, and they were
      humbled
   by oppression, calamity and sorrow;
40 he who pours contempt on nobles
   made them wander in a trackless waste.
41 But he lifted the needy out of their affliction
   and increased their families like flocks.
42 The upright see and rejoice,
   but all the wicked shut their mouths.

43 Whoever is wise, let him heed these things
   and consider the great love of the Lord.

Psalm 137

1   By the rivers of Babylon we sat and wept
        when we remembered Zion.
2   There on the poplars
        we hung our harps,
3   for there our captors asked us for songs,
        our tormentors demanded songs of joy;
        they said, "Sing us one of the songs of Zion!"

4   How can we sing the songs of the Lord
        while in a foreign land?
5   If I forget you, O Jerusalem,
        may my right hand forget its skill.
6   May my tongue cling to the roof of my mouth
        if I do not remember you,
        if I do not consider Jerusalem
        my highest joy.

7   Remember, O Lord, what the Edomites did
        on the day Jerusalem fell.
  "Tear it down," they cried,
        "tear it down to its foundations!"

8   O Daughter of Babylon, doomed to destruction,
        happy is he who repays you
        for what you have done to us—
9   he who seizes your infants
        and dashes them against the rocks.

Proverbs 17

1   Better a dry crust with peace and quiet
        than a house full of feasting, [a] with strife.

---

[a]1 Hebrew *sacrifices*

2 A wise servant will rule over a disgraceful son,
and will share the inheritance as one of the
brothers.

3 The crucible for silver and the furnace for gold,
but the Lord tests the heart.

4 A wicked man listens to evil lips;
a liar pays attention to a malicious tongue.

5 He who mocks the poor shows contempt
for their Maker;
whoever gloats over disaster will not go
unpunished.

6 Children's children are a crown to the aged,
and parents are the pride of their children.

7 Arrogant *a* lips are unsuited to a fool—
how much worse lying lips to a ruler!

8 A bribe is a charm to the one who gives it;
wherever he turns, he succeeds.

9 He who covers over an offense promotes love,
but whoever repeats the matter separates
close friends.

10 A rebuke impresses a man of discernment
more than a hundred lashes a fool.

11 An evil man is bent only on rebellion;
a merciless official will be sent against him.

12 Better to meet a bear robbed of her cubs
than a fool in his folly.

a7 Or *Eloquent*

13 If a man pays back evil for good,
   evil will never leave his house.

14 Starting a quarrel is like breaching a dam;
   so drop the matter before a dispute breaks out.

15 Acquitting the guilty and condemning the
         innocent—
   the Lord detests them both.

16 Of what use is money in the hand of a fool,
   since he has no desire to get wisdom?

17 A friend loves at all times,
   and a brother is born for adversity.

18 A man lacking in judgment strikes hands in
         pledge
   and puts up security for his neighbor.

19 He who loves a quarrel loves sin;
   he who builds a high gate invites destruction.

20 A man of perverse heart does not prosper;
   he whose tongue is deceitful falls into trouble.

21 To have a fool for a son brings grief;
   there is no joy for the father of a fool.

22 A cheerful heart is good medicine,
   but a crushed spirit dries up the bones.

23 A wicked man accepts a bribe in secret
   to pervert the course of justice.

24 A discerning man keeps wisdom in view,
   but a fool's eyes wander to the ends of the earth.

25 A foolish son brings grief to his father
   and bitterness to the one who bore him.

26 It is not good to punish an innocent man,
   or to flog officials for their integrity.

27 A man of knowledge uses words with restraint,
   and a man of understanding is even-tempered.

28 Even a fool is thought wise if he keeps silent,
   and discerning if he holds his tongue.

DAY 18

Psalm 18

For the director of music. Of David the servant of the
Lord. He sang to the Lord the words of this song
when the Lord delivered him from the hand of all his
enemies and from the hand of Saul. He said:

1 I love you, O Lord, my strength.

2 The Lord is my rock, my fortress and my deliverer;
   my God is my rock, in whom I take refuge.
   He is my shield and the horn *a* of my salvation,
      my stronghold.

3 I call to the Lord, who is worthy of praise,
   and I am saved from my enemies.

4 The cords of death entangled me;
   the torrents of destruction overwhelmed me.

5 The cords of the grave *b* coiled around me;
   the snares of death confronted me.

6 In my distress I called to the Lord;
   I cried to my God for help.
   From his temple he heard my voice;
      my cry came before him, into his ears.

---

*a*2 *Horn* here symbolizes strength.   *b*5 Hebrew *Sheol*

7   The earth trembled and quaked,
        and the foundations of the mountains shook;
        they trembled because he was angry.
8   Smoke rose from his nostrils;
        consuming fire came from his mouth,
        burning coals blazed out of it.
9   He parted the heavens and came down;
        dark clouds were under his feet.
10 He mounted the cherubim and flew;
        he soared on the wings of the wind.
11 He made darkness his covering, his canopy
            around him—
        the dark rain clouds of the sky.
12 Out of the brightness of his presence clouds
            advanced,
        with hailstones and bolts of lightning.
13 The Lord thundered from heaven;
        the voice of the Most High resounded. *a*
14 He shot his arrows and scattered the enemies,
        great bolts of lightning and routed them.
15 The valleys of the sea were exposed
        and the foundations of the earth laid bare
    at your rebuke, O Lord,
        at the blast of breath from your nostrils.

16 He reached down from on high and took hold of me;
        he drew me out of deep waters.
17 He rescued me from my powerful enemy,
        from my foes, who were too strong for me.
18 They confronted me in the day of my disaster,

---

*a*13 Some Hebrew manuscripts and Septuagint (see also 2 Samuel 22:14); most Hebrew manuscripts *resounded, / amid hailstones and bolts of lightning*

but the Lord was my support.
19 He brought me out into a spacious place;
    he rescued me because he delighted in me.
20 The Lord has dealt with me according to my
        righteousness;
    according to the cleanness of my hands he has
        rewarded me.
21 For I have kept the ways of the Lord;
    I have not done evil by turning from my God.
22 All his laws are before me;
    I have not turned away from his decrees.
23 I have been blameless before him
    and have kept myself from sin.
24 The Lord has rewarded me according to my
        righteousness,
    according to the cleanness of my hands in his sight.

25 To the faithful you show yourself faithful,
    to the blameless you show yourself blameless,
26 to the pure you show yourself pure,
    but to the crooked you show yourself shrewd.
27 You save the humble
    but bring low those whose eyes are haughty.
28 You, O Lord, keep my lamp burning;
    my God turns my darkness into light.
29 With your help I can advance against a troop [a];
    with my God I can scale a wall.

30 As for God, his way is perfect;
    the word of the Lord is flawless.
    He is a shield
    for all who take refuge in him.
31 For who is God besides the Lord?

[a]29 Or *can run through a barricade*

And who is the Rock except our God?
32 It is God who arms me with strength
and makes my way perfect.
33 He makes my feet like the feet of a deer;
he enables me to stand on the heights.
34 He trains my hands for battle;
my arms can bend a bow of bronze.
35 You give me your shield of victory,
and your right hand sustains me;
you stoop down to make me great.
36 You broaden the path beneath me,
so that my ankles do not turn.

37 I pursued my enemies and overtook them;
I did not turn back till they were destroyed.
38 I crushed them so that they could not rise;
they fell beneath my feet.
39 You armed me with strength for battle;
you made my adversaries bow at my feet.
40 You made my enemies turn their backs in flight,
and I destroyed my foes.
41 They cried for help, but there was no one
to save them—
to the Lord, but he did not answer.
42 I beat them as fine as dust borne on the wind;
I poured them out like mud in the streets.

43 You have delivered me from the attacks
of the people;
you have made me the head of nations;
people I did not know are subject to me.
44 As soon as they hear me, they obey me;
foreigners cringe before me.
45 They all lose heart;
they come trembling from their strongholds.

46 The Lord lives! Praise be to my Rock!
      Exalted be God my Savior!
47 He is the God who avenges me,
      who subdues nations under me,
48 who saves me from my enemies.
    You exalted me above my foes;
      from violent men you rescued me.
49 Therefore I will praise you among the nations,
          O Lord;
      I will sing praises to your name.
50 He gives his king great victories;
      he shows unfailing kindness to his anointed,
      to David and his descendants forever.

Psalm 48

A song. A psalm of the Sons of Korah.

1 Great is the Lord, and most worthy of praise,
      in the city of our God, his holy mountain.
2 It is beautiful in its loftiness,
      the joy of the whole earth.
    Like the utmost heights of Zaphon *a* is Mount Zion,
      the *b* city of the Great King.
3 God is in her citadels;
      he has shown himself to be her fortress.

4 When the kings joined forces,
      when they advanced together,
5 they saw her and were astounded;
      they fled in terror.
6 Trembling seized them there,

---

*a*2 *Zaphon* can refer to a sacred mountain or the direction north.
*b*2 Or *earth,* / *Mount Zion, on the northern side* / *of the*

      pain like that of a woman in labor.
7 You destroyed them like ships of Tarshish
      shattered by an east wind.

8 As we have heard,
      so have we seen
  in the city of the Lord Almighty,
      in the city of our God:
      God makes her secure forever.   *Selah*

9 Within your temple, O God,
      we meditate on your unfailing love.
10 Like your name, O God,
      your praise reaches to the ends of the earth;
      your right hand is filled with righteousness.
11 Mount Zion rejoices,
      the villages of Judah are glad
      because of your judgments.

12 Walk about Zion, go around her,
      count her towers,
13 consider well her ramparts,
      view her citadels,
      that you may tell of them to the next generation.
14 For this God is our God for ever and ever;
      he will be our guide even to the end.

Psalm 78
A *maskil* [a] of Asaph.

1 O my people, hear my teaching;
      listen to the words of my mouth.
2 I will open my mouth in parables,

---

[a] Title: Probably a literary or musical term

I will utter hidden things, things from of old—
3   what we have heard and known,
    what our fathers have told us.
4   We will not hide them from their children;
    we will tell the next generation
the praiseworthy deeds of the Lord,
  his power, and the wonders he has done.
5   He decreed statutes for Jacob
    and established the law in Israel,
which he commanded our forefathers
  to teach their children,
6   so the next generation would know them,
    even the children yet to be born,
    and they in turn would tell their children.
7   Then they would put their trust in God
    and would not forget his deeds
    but would keep his commands.
8   They would not be like their forefathers—
    a stubborn and rebellious generation,
whose hearts were not loyal to God,
  whose spirits were not faithful to him.

9   The men of Ephraim, though armed with bows,
    turned back on the day of battle;
10   they did not keep God's covenant
    and refused to live by his law.
11   They forgot what he had done,
    the wonders he had shown them.
12   He did miracles in the sight of their fathers
    in the land of Egypt, in the region of Zoan.
13   He divided the sea and led them through;
    he made the water stand firm like a wall.
14   He guided them with the cloud by day
    and with light from the fire all night.

15 He split the rocks in the desert
     and gave them water as abundant as the seas;
16 he brought streams out of a rocky crag
     and made water flow down like rivers.

17 But they continued to sin against him,
     rebelling in the desert against the Most High.
18 They willfully put God to the test
     by demanding the food they craved.
19 They spoke against God, saying,
     "Can God spread a table in the desert?
20 When he struck the rock, water gushed out,
     and streams flowed abundantly.
     But can he also give us food?
     Can he supply meat for his people?"
21 When the Lord heard them, he was very angry;
     his fire broke out against Jacob,
     and his wrath rose against Israel,
22 for they did not believe in God
     or trust in his deliverance.
23 Yet he gave a command to the skies above
     and opened the doors of the heavens;
24 he rained down manna for the people to eat,
     he gave them the grain of heaven.
25 Men ate the bread of angels;
     he sent them all the food they could eat.
26 He let loose the east wind from the heavens
     and led forth the south wind by his power.
27 He rained meat down on them like dust,
     flying birds like sand on the seashore.
28 He made them come down inside their camp,
     all around their tents.
29 They ate till they had more than enough,
     for he had given them what they craved.

30 But before they turned from the food they craved,
   even while it was still in their mouths,
31 God's anger rose against them;
   he put to death the sturdiest among them,
   cutting down the young men of Israel.

32 In spite of all this, they kept on sinning;
   in spite of his wonders, they did not believe.
33 So he ended their days in futility
   and their years in terror.
34 Whenever God slew them, they would seek him;
   they eagerly turned to him again.
35 They remembered that God was their Rock,
   that God Most High was their Redeemer.
36 But then they would flatter him with their mouths,
   lying to him with their tongues;
37 their hearts were not loyal to him,
   they were not faithful to his covenant.
38 Yet he was merciful;
   he forgave their iniquities
   and did not destroy them.
   Time after time he restrained his anger
   and did not stir up his full wrath.
39 He remembered that they were but flesh,
   a passing breeze that does not return.

40 How often they rebelled against him in the desert
   and grieved him in the wasteland!
41 Again and again they put God to the test;
   they vexed the Holy One of Israel.
42 They did not remember his power—
   the day he redeemed them from the oppressor,
43 the day he displayed his miraculous signs in
      Egypt,
   his wonders in the region of Zoan.

44 He turned their rivers to blood;
  they could not drink from their streams.
45 He sent swarms of flies that devoured them,
  and frogs that devastated them.
46 He gave their crops to the grasshopper,
  their produce to the locust.
47 He destroyed their vines with hail
  and their sycamore-figs with sleet.
48 He gave over their cattle to the hail,
  their livestock to bolts of lightning.
49 He unleashed against them his hot anger,
  his wrath, indignation and hostility—
  a band of destroying angels.
50 He prepared a path for his anger;
  he did not spare them from death
  but gave them over to the plague.
51 He struck down all the firstborn of Egypt,
  the firstfruits of manhood in the tents of Ham.
52 But he brought his people out like a flock;
  he led them like sheep through the desert.
53 He guided them safely, so they were unafraid;
  but the sea engulfed their enemies.
54 Thus he brought them to the border of his holy land,
  to the hill country his right hand had taken.
55 He drove out nations before them
  and allotted their lands to them as an
      inheritance;
  he settled the tribes of Israel in their homes.

56 But they put God to the test
  and rebelled against the Most High;
  they did not keep his statutes.
57 Like their fathers they were disloyal and faithless,
  as unreliable as a faulty bow.

58 They angered him with their high places;
    they aroused his jealousy with their idols.
59 When God heard them, he was very angry;
    he rejected Israel completely.
60 He abandoned the tabernacle of Shiloh,
    the tent he had set up among men.
61 He sent the ark of his might into captivity,
    his splendor into the hands of the enemy.
62 He gave his people over to the sword;
    he was very angry with his inheritance.
63 Fire consumed their young men,
    and their maidens had no wedding songs;
64 their priests were put to the sword,
    and their widows could not weep.

65 Then the Lord awoke as from sleep,
    as a man wakes from the stupor of wine.
66 He beat back his enemies;
    he put them to everlasting shame.
67 Then he rejected the tents of Joseph,
    he did not choose the tribe of Ephraim;
68 but he chose the tribe of Judah,
    Mount Zion, which he loved.
69 He built his sanctuary like the heights,
    like the earth that he established forever.
70 He chose David his servant
    and took him from the sheep pens;
71 from tending the sheep he brought him
    to be the shepherd of his people Jacob,
    of Israel his inheritance.
72 And David shepherded them with integrity of
      heart;
    with skillful hands he led them.

Psalm 108

A song. A psalm of David.

1   My heart is steadfast, O God;
        I will sing and make music with all my soul.
2   Awake, harp and lyre!
        I will awaken the dawn.
3   I will praise you, O Lord, among the nations;
        I will sing of you among the peoples.
4   For great is your love, higher than the heavens;
        your faithfulness reaches to the skies.
5   Be exalted, O God, above the heavens,
        and let your glory be over all the earth.

6   Save us and help us with your right hand,
        that those you love may be delivered.
7   God has spoken from his sanctuary:
        "In triumph I will parcel out Shechem
        and measure off the Valley of Succoth.
8   Gilead is mine, Manasseh is mine;
        Ephraim is my helmet,
        Judah my scepter.
9   Moab is my washbasin,
        upon Edom I toss my sandal;
        over Philistia I shout in triumph."

10   Who will bring me to the fortified city?
        Who will lead me to Edom?
11   Is it not you, O God, you who have rejected us
        and no longer go out with our armies?
12   Give us aid against the enemy,
        for the help of man is worthless.
13   With God we will gain the victory,
        and he will trample down our enemies.

Psalm 138
Of David.

1. I will praise you, O Lord, with all my heart;
     before the "gods" I will sing your praise.
2. I will bow down toward your holy temple
     and will praise your name
     for your love and your faithfulness,
   for you have exalted above all things
     your name and your word.
3. When I called, you answered me;
     you made me bold and stouthearted.

4. May all the kings of the earth praise you, O Lord,
     when they hear the words of your mouth.
5. May they sing of the ways of the Lord,
     for the glory of the Lord is great.

6. Though the Lord is on high, he looks upon the lowly,
     but the proud he knows from afar.
7. Though I walk in the midst of trouble,
     you preserve my life;
   you stretch out your hand against the anger of my
        foes,
     with your right hand you save me.
8. The Lord will fulfill his purpose for me;
     your love, O Lord, endures forever—
     do not abandon the works of your hands.

Proverbs 18

1. An unfriendly man pursues selfish ends;
     he defies all sound judgment.

2. A fool finds no pleasure in understanding
     but delights in airing his own opinions.

3   When wickedness comes, so does contempt,
        and with shame comes disgrace.

4   The words of a man's mouth are deep waters,
        but the fountain of wisdom is a bubbling brook.

5   It is not good to be partial to the wicked
        or to deprive the innocent of justice.

6   A fool's lips bring him strife,
        and his mouth invites a beating.

7   A fool's mouth is his undoing,
        and his lips are a snare to his soul.

8   The words of a gossip are like choice morsels;
        they go down to a man's inmost parts.

9   One who is slack in his work
        is brother to one who destroys.

10 The name of the Lord is a strong tower;
        the righteous run to it and are safe.

11 The wealth of the rich is their fortified city;
        they imagine it an unscalable wall.

12 Before his downfall a man's heart is proud,
        but humility comes before honor.

13 He who answers before listening—
        that is his folly and his shame.

14 A man's spirit sustains him in sickness,
        but a crushed spirit who can bear?

15 The heart of the discerning acquires
            knowledge;
        the ears of the wise seek it out.

16 A gift opens the way for the giver
   and ushers him into the presence of the great.

17 The first to present his case seems right,
   till another comes forward and questions him.

18 Casting the lot settles disputes
   and keeps strong opponents apart.

19 An offended brother is more unyielding than a
      fortified city,
   and disputes are like the barred gates of a citadel.

20 From the fruit of his mouth a man's stomach is filled;
   with the harvest from his lips he is satisfied.

21 The tongue has the power of life and death,
   and those who love it will eat its fruit.

22 He who finds a wife finds what is good
   and receives favor from the Lord.

23 A poor man pleads for mercy,
   but a rich man answers harshly.

24 A man of many companions may come to ruin,
   but there is a friend who sticks closer than a
      brother.

DAY 19

Psalm 19
For the director of music. A psalm of David.

1 The heavens declare the glory of God;
   the skies proclaim the work of his hands.

2 Day after day they pour forth speech;

night after night they display knowledge.
3 There is no speech or language
     where their voice is not heard. *a*
4 Their voice *b* goes out into all the earth,
     their words to the ends of the world.

In the heavens he has pitched a tent for the sun,
5   which is like a bridegroom coming forth from
          his pavilion,
     like a champion rejoicing to run his course.
6 It rises at one end of the heavens
     and makes its circuit to the other;
     nothing is hidden from its heat.

7 The law of the Lord is perfect,
     reviving the soul.
  The statutes of the Lord are trustworthy,
     making wise the simple.
8 The precepts of the Lord are right,
     giving joy to the heart.
  The commands of the Lord are radiant,
     giving light to the eyes.
9 The fear of the Lord is pure,
     enduring forever.
  The ordinances of the Lord are sure
     and altogether righteous.
10 They are more precious than gold,
     than much pure gold;
   they are sweeter than honey,
     than honey from the comb.
11 By them is your servant warned;
     in keeping them there is great reward.

---

*a*3 Or *They have no speech, there are no words; / no sound is heard from them*   *b*4 Septuagint, Jerome and Syriac; Hebrew *line*

12 Who can discern his errors?
        Forgive my hidden faults.
13 Keep your servant also from willful sins;
        may they not rule over me.
    Then will I be blameless,
        innocent of great transgression.

14 May the words of my mouth
            and the meditation of my heart
        be pleasing in your sight,
        O Lord, my Rock and my Redeemer.

Psalm 49

For the director of music. Of the Sons of Korah.
A psalm.

1 Hear this, all you peoples;
        listen, all who live in this world,
2 both low and high,
        rich and poor alike:
3 My mouth will speak words of wisdom;
        the utterance from my heart will give
            understanding.
4 I will turn my ear to a proverb;
        with the harp I will expound my riddle:

5 Why should I fear when evil days come,
        when wicked deceivers surround me—
6 those who trust in their wealth
        and boast of their great riches?
7 No man can redeem the life of another
        or give to God a ransom for him—
8 the ransom for a life is costly,
        no payment is ever enough—

9   that he should live on forever
         and not see decay.

10   For all can see that wise men die;
         the foolish and the senseless alike perish
         and leave their wealth to others.

11   Their tombs will remain their houses *a* forever,
         their dwellings for endless generations,
         though they had *b* named lands after themselves.

12   But man, despite his riches, does not endure;
         he is *c* like the beasts that perish.

13   This is the fate of those who trust in themselves,
         and of their followers, who approve their
                 sayings.   *Selah*

14   Like sheep they are destined for the grave, *d*
         and death will feed on them.
     The upright will rule over them in the morning;
         their forms will decay in the grave, *e*
         far from their princely mansions.

15   But God will redeem my life *f* from the grave;
         he will surely take me to himself.   *Selah*

16   Do not be overawed when a man grows rich,
         when the splendor of his house increases;

17   for he will take nothing with him when he dies,
         his splendor will not descend with him.

18   Though while he lived he counted himself
                 blessed—
         and men praise you when you prosper—

---

*a*11 Septuagint and Syriac; Hebrew *In their thoughts their houses will
remain*   *b*11 Or */for they have*   *c*12 Hebrew; Septuagint and
Syriac read verse 12 the same as verse 20.   *d*14 Hebrew *Sheol*; also
in verse 15   *e*14 Hebrew *Sheol*; also in verse 15   *f*15 Or *soul*

19 he will join the generation of his fathers,
    who will never see the light of life.

20 A man who has riches without understanding
    is like the beasts that perish.

Psalm 79

A psalm of Asaph.

1   O God, the nations have invaded your inheritance;
    they have defiled your holy temple,
        they have reduced Jerusalem to rubble.

2   They have given the dead bodies of your servants
    as food to the birds of the air,
        the flesh of your saints to the beasts of the earth.

3   They have poured out blood like water
    all around Jerusalem,
        and there is no one to bury the dead.

4   We are objects of reproach to our neighbors,
    of scorn and derision to those around us.

5   How long, O Lord? Will you be angry forever?
    How long will your jealousy burn like fire?

6   Pour out your wrath on the nations
    that do not acknowledge you,
        on the kingdoms
    that do not call on your name;

7   for they have devoured Jacob
    and destroyed his homeland.

8   Do not hold against us the sins of the fathers;
    may your mercy come quickly to meet us,
        for we are in desperate need.

9   Help us, O God our Savior,
    for the glory of your name;

deliver us and forgive our sins
  for your name's sake.
10 Why should the nations say,
    "Where is their God?"
  Before our eyes, make known among the
      nations
    that you avenge the outpoured blood
      of your servants.
11 May the groans of the prisoners come
      before you;
    by the strength of your arm
    preserve those condemned to die.

12 Pay back into the laps of our neighbors
      seven times
    the reproach they have hurled at you,
      O Lord.
13 Then we your people, the sheep of your
      pasture,
    will praise you forever;
  from generation to generation
    we will recount your praise.

Psalm 109

For the director of music. Of David. A psalm.

1 O God, whom I praise,
    do not remain silent,
2 for wicked and deceitful men
    have opened their mouths against me;
    they have spoken against me with lying
      tongues.
3 With words of hatred they surround me;
    they attack me without cause.

4 In return for my friendship they accuse me,
    but I am a man of prayer.
5 They repay me evil for good,
    and hatred for my friendship.

6 Appoint ^{a} an evil man ^{b} to oppose him;
    let an accuser ^{c} stand at his right hand.
7 When he is tried, let him be found guilty,
    and may his prayers condemn him.
8 May his days be few;
    may another take his place of leadership.
9 May his children be fatherless
    and his wife a widow.
10 May his children be wandering beggars;
    may they be driven ^{d} from their ruined homes.
11 May a creditor seize all he has;
    may strangers plunder the fruits of his labor.
12 May no one extend kindness to him
    or take pity on his fatherless children.
13 May his descendants be cut off,
    their names blotted out from the next generation.
14 May the iniquity of his fathers be remembered
    before the Lord;
    may the sin of his mother never be blotted out.
15 May their sins always remain before the Lord,
    that he may cut off the memory of them from
    the earth.

16 For he never thought of doing a kindness,
    but hounded to death the poor
    and the needy and the brokenhearted.
17 He loved to pronounce a curse—

^{a}6 Or *They say: "Appoint* (with quotation marks at the end of verse 19) ^{b}6 Or *the Evil One* ^{c}6 Or *let Satan* ^{d}10 Septuagint; Hebrew *sought*

may it ^a come on him;
he found no pleasure in blessing—
   may it be ^b far from him.

18 He wore cursing as his garment;
   it entered into his body like water,
   into his bones like oil.

19 May it be like a cloak wrapped about him,
   like a belt tied forever around him.

20 May this be the Lord's payment to my accusers,
   to those who speak evil of me.

21 But you, O Sovereign Lord,
   deal well with me for your name's sake;
   out of the goodness of your love, deliver me.

22 For I am poor and needy,
   and my heart is wounded within me.

23 I fade away like an evening shadow;
   I am shaken off like a locust.

24 My knees give way from fasting;
   my body is thin and gaunt.

25 I am an object of scorn to my accusers;
   when they see me, they shake their heads.

26 Help me, O Lord my God;
   save me in accordance with your love.

27 Let them know that it is your hand,
   that you, O Lord, have done it.

28 They may curse, but you will bless;
   when they attack they will be put to shame,
   but your servant will rejoice.

29 My accusers will be clothed with disgrace
   and wrapped in shame as in a cloak.

^a17 Or *curse, / and it has*   ^a17 Or *blessing, / and it is*

30 With my mouth I will greatly extol the Lord;
   in the great throng I will praise him.
31 For he stands at the right hand of the needy one,
   to save his life from those who condemn him.

Psalm 139

For the director of music. Of David. A psalm.

1 O Lord, you have searched me
   and you know me.
2 You know when I sit and when I rise;
   you perceive my thoughts from afar.
3 You discern my going out and my lying down;
   you are familiar with all my ways.
4 Before a word is on my tongue
   you know it completely, O Lord.

5 You hem me in—behind and before;
   you have laid your hand upon me.
6 Such knowledge is too wonderful for me,
   too lofty for me to attain.

7 Where can I go from your Spirit?
   Where can I flee from your presence?
8 If I go up to the heavens, you are there;
   if I make my bed in the depths, *a* you are there.
9 If I rise on the wings of the dawn,
   if I settle on the far side of the sea,
10 even there your hand will guide me,
    your right hand will hold me fast.

11 If I say, "Surely the darkness will hide me
    and the light become night around me,"

a8 Hebrew *Sheol*

12 even the darkness will not be dark to you;
    the night will shine like the day,
    for darkness is as light to you.

13 For you created my inmost being;
    you knit me together in my mother's womb.
14 I praise you because I am fearfully and
        wonderfully made;
    your works are wonderful,
    I know that full well.
15 My frame was not hidden from you
    when I was made in the secret place.
    When I was woven together in the depths
        of the earth,
16 your eyes saw my unformed body.
    All the days ordained for me
        were written in your book
        before one of them came to be.

17 How precious to *a* me are your thoughts,
        O God!
    How vast is the sum of them!
18 Were I to count them,
        they would outnumber the grains of sand.
    When I awake,
        I am still with you.

19 If only you would slay the wicked, O God!
        Away from me, you bloodthirsty men!
20 They speak of you with evil intent;
        your adversaries misuse your name.
21 Do I not hate those who hate you, O Lord,
        and abhor those who rise up against you?

*a*17 Or *concerning*

22 I have nothing but hatred for them;
       I count them my enemies.

23 Search me, O God, and know my heart;
       test me and know my anxious thoughts.

24 See if there is any offensive way in me,
       and lead me in the way everlasting.

Proverbs 19

1 Better a poor man whose walk is blameless
      than a fool whose lips are perverse.

2 It is not good to have zeal without knowledge,
      nor to be hasty and miss the way.

3 A man's own folly ruins his life,
      yet his heart rages against the Lord.

4 Wealth brings many friends,
      but a poor man's friend deserts him.

5 A false witness will not go unpunished,
      and he who pours out lies will not go free.

6 Many curry favor with a ruler,
      and everyone is the friend of a man
         who gives gifts.

7 A poor man is shunned by all his relatives—
      how much more do his friends avoid him!
   Though he pursues them with pleading,
      they are nowhere to be found. *a*

8 He who gets wisdom loves his own soul;
      he who cherishes understanding prospers.

---

*a*7 The meaning of the Hebrew for this sentence is uncertain.

9 A false witness will not go unpunished,
    and he who pours out lies will perish.

10 It is not fitting for a fool to live in luxury—
    how much worse for a slave to rule over
        princes!

11 A man's wisdom gives him patience;
    it is to his glory to overlook an offense.

12 A king's rage is like the roar of a lion,
    but his favor is like dew on the grass.

13 A foolish son is his father's ruin,
    and a quarrelsome wife is like a constant
        dripping.

14 Houses and wealth are inherited from parents,
    but a prudent wife is from the Lord.

15 Laziness brings on deep sleep,
    and the shiftless man goes hungry.

16 He who obeys instructions guards his life,
    but he who is contemptuous of his ways will die.

17 He who is kind to the poor lends to the Lord,
    and he will reward him for what he has done.

18 Discipline your son, for in that there is hope;
    do not be a willing party to his death.

19 A hot-tempered man must pay the penalty;
    if you rescue him, you will have to do it again.

20 Listen to advice and accept instruction,
    and in the end you will be wise.

21 Many are the plans in a man's heart,
    but it is the Lord's purpose that prevails.

22 What a man desires is unfailing love *a*;
   better to be poor than a liar.

23 The fear of the Lord leads to life:
   Then one rests content, untouched by trouble.

24 The sluggard buries his hand in the dish;
   he will not even bring it back to his mouth!

25 Flog a mocker, and the simple will learn prudence;
   rebuke a discerning man, and he will
      gain knowledge.

26 He who robs his father and drives out his mother
   is a son who brings shame and disgrace.

27 Stop listening to instruction, my son,
   and you will stray from the words of
      knowledge.

28 A corrupt witness mocks at justice,
   and the mouth of the wicked gulps down evil.

29 Penalties are prepared for mockers,
   and beatings for the backs of fools.

DAY 20

Psalm 20
For the director of music. A psalm of David.

1 May the Lord answer you when you are
      in distress;
   may the name of the God of Jacob protect you.

2 May he send you help from the sanctuary

a22 Or A man's greed is his shame

and grant you support from Zion.
3 May he remember all your sacrifices
and accept your burnt offerings.   *Selah*
4 May he give you the desire of your heart
and make all your plans succeed.
5 We will shout for joy when you are victorious
and will lift up our banners in the name
of our God.
May the Lord grant all your requests.

6 Now I know that the Lord saves his anointed;
he answers him from his holy heaven
with the saving power of his right hand.
7 Some trust in chariots and some in horses,
but we trust in the name of the Lord our God.
8 They are brought to their knees and fall,
but we rise up and stand firm.

9 O Lord, save the king!
Answer *a* us when we call!

Psalm 50

A psalm of Asaph.

1 The Mighty One, God, the Lord,
speaks and summons the earth
from the rising of the sun to the place where it
sets.
2 From Zion, perfect in beauty,
God shines forth.
3 Our God comes and will not be silent;
a fire devours before him,
and around him a tempest rages.

*a*9 Or *save! / O King, answer*

4   He summons the heavens above,
      and the earth, that he may judge his people:
5   "Gather to me my consecrated ones,
      who made a covenant with me by sacrifice."
6   And the heavens proclaim his righteousness,
      for God himself is judge.   *Selah*

7   "Hear, O my people, and I will speak,
      O Israel, and I will testify against you:
      I am God, your God.
8   I do not rebuke you for your sacrifices
      or your burnt offerings, which are ever before
        me.
9   I have no need of a bull from your stall
      or of goats from your pens,
10 for every animal of the forest is mine,
      and the cattle on a thousand hills.
11 I know every bird in the mountains,
      and the creatures of the field are mine.
12 If I were hungry I would not tell you,
      for the world is mine, and all that is in it.
13 Do I eat the flesh of bulls
      or drink the blood of goats?
14 Sacrifice thank offerings to God,
      fulfill your vows to the Most High,
15 and call upon me in the day of trouble;
      I will deliver you, and you will honor me."

16 But to the wicked, God says:

  "What right have you to recite my laws
      or take my covenant on your lips?
17 You hate my instruction
      and cast my words behind you.
18 When you see a thief, you join with him;

you throw in your lot with adulterers.
19 You use your mouth for evil
   and harness your tongue to deceit.
20 You speak continually against your brother
   and slander your own mother's son.
21 These things you have done and I kept silent;
   you thought I was altogether *a* like you.
   But I will rebuke you
   and accuse you to your face.

22 Consider this, you who forget God,
   or I will tear you to pieces, with none to rescue:
23 He who sacrifices thank offerings honors me,
   and he prepares the way
   so that I may show him *b* the salvation of God."

Psalm 80
For the director of music. To the tune of
"The Lilies of the Covenant." Of Asaph. A psalm.

1 Hear us, O Shepherd of Israel,
   you who lead Joseph like a flock;
   you who sit enthroned between the cherubim,
      shine forth
2   before Ephraim, Benjamin and Manasseh.
   Awaken your might;
   come and save us.

3 Restore us, O God;
   make your face shine upon us,
   that we may be saved.
4 O Lord God Almighty,

*a*21 Or *thought the 'I am' was*   *b*23 Or *and to him who considers his
way / I will show*

how long will your anger smolder
against the prayers of your people?

5   You have fed them with the bread of tears;
    you have made them drink tears by the bowlful.

6   You have made us a source of contention
          to our neighbors,
    and our enemies mock us.

7   Restore us, O God Almighty;
    make your face shine upon us,
    that we may be saved.

8   You brought a vine out of Egypt;
    you drove out the nations and planted it.

9   You cleared the ground for it,
    and it took root and filled the land.

10 The mountains were covered with its shade,
    the mighty cedars with its branches.

11 It sent out its boughs to the Sea, *a*
    its shoots as far as the River. *b*

12 Why have you broken down its walls
    so that all who pass by pick its grapes?

13 Boars from the forest ravage it
    and the creatures of the field feed on it.

14 Return to us, O God Almighty!
    Look down from heaven and see!
    Watch over this vine,

15   the root your right hand has planted,
    the son *c* you have raised up for yourself.

16 Your vine is cut down, it is burned with fire;
    at your rebuke your people perish.

---

*a*11 Probably the Mediterranean   *b*11 That is, the Euphrates
*c*15 Or *branch*

17 Let your hand rest on the man at your right hand,
the son of man you have raised up for
yourself.
18 Then we will not turn away from you;
revive us, and we will call on your name.

19 Restore us, O Lord God Almighty;
make your face shine upon us,
that we may be saved.

Psalm 110
Of David. A psalm.

1 The Lord says to my Lord:
"Sit at my right hand
until I make your enemies
a footstool for your feet."

2 The Lord will extend your mighty scepter from
Zion;
you will rule in the midst of your enemies.
3 Your troops will be willing
on your day of battle.
Arrayed in holy majesty,
from the womb of the dawn
you will receive the dew of your youth. *a*

4 The Lord has sworn
and will not change his mind:
"You are a priest forever,
in the order of Melchizedek."

5 The Lord is at your right hand;
he will crush kings on the day of his wrath.

a3 Or / your young men will come to you like the dew

6   He will judge the nations, heaping up the dead
         and crushing the rulers of the whole earth.
7   He will drink from a brook beside the way *a*;
         therefore he will lift up his head.

Psalm 140

For the director of music. A psalm of David.

1   Rescue me, O Lord, from evil men;
         protect me from men of violence,
2   who devise evil plans in their hearts
         and stir up war every day.
3   They make their tongues as sharp as
             a serpent's;
         the poison of vipers is on their lips.   *Selah*

4   Keep me, O Lord, from the hands of the wicked;
         protect me from men of violence
         who plan to trip my feet.
5   Proud men have hidden a snare for me;
         they have spread out the cords of their net
         and have set traps for me along my path.   *Selah*

6   O Lord, I say to you, "You are my God."
         Hear, O Lord, my cry for mercy.
7   O Sovereign Lord, my strong deliverer,
         who shields my head in the day of battle—
8   do not grant the wicked their desires, O Lord;
         do not let their plans succeed,
         or they will become proud.   *Selah*

9   Let the heads of those who surround me
         be covered with the trouble their lips have caused.

*a*7 Or / *The One who grants succession will set him in authority*

10 Let burning coals fall upon them;
    may they be thrown into the fire,
    into miry pits, never to rise.
11 Let slanderers not be established in the land;
    may disaster hunt down men of violence.

12 I know that the Lord secures justice for the poor
    and upholds the cause of the needy.
13 Surely the righteous will praise your name
    and the upright will live before you.

Proverbs 20

1 Wine is a mocker and beer a brawler;
    whoever is led astray by them is not wise.
2 A king's wrath is like the roar of a lion;
    he who angers him forfeits his life.
3 It is to a man's honor to avoid strife,
    but every fool is quick to quarrel.
4 A sluggard does not plow in season;
    so at harvest time he looks but finds
        nothing.
5 The purposes of a man's heart are deep waters,
    but a man of understanding draws them out.
6 Many a man claims to have unfailing love,
    but a faithful man who can find?
7 The righteous man leads a blameless life;
    blessed are his children after him.
8 When a king sits on his throne to judge,
    he winnows out all evil with his eyes.

DAY 20

9   Who can say, "I have kept my heart pure;
        I am clean and without sin"?

10 Differing weights and differing measures—
        the Lord detests them both.

11 Even a child is known by his actions,
        by whether his conduct is pure and right.

12 Ears that hear and eyes that see—
        the Lord has made them both.

13 Do not love sleep or you will grow poor;
        stay awake and you will have food to spare.

14 "It's no good, it's no good!" says the buyer;
        then off he goes and boasts about his purchase.

15 Gold there is, and rubies in abundance,
        but lips that speak knowledge are a rare jewel.

16 Take the garment of one who puts up security for
            a stranger;
        hold it in pledge if he does it for a wayward
            woman.

17 Food gained by fraud tastes sweet to a man,
        but he ends up with a mouth full of gravel.

18 Make plans by seeking advice;
        if you wage war, obtain guidance.

19 A gossip betrays a confidence;
        so avoid a man who talks too much.

20 If a man curses his father or mother,
        his lamp will be snuffed out in pitch darkness.

21 An inheritance quickly gained at the beginning
        will not be blessed at the end.

22 Do not say, "I'll pay you back for this wrong!"
    Wait for the Lord, and he will deliver you.

23 The Lord detests differing weights,
    and dishonest scales do not please him.

24 A man's steps are directed by the Lord.
    How then can anyone understand his own way?

25 It is a trap for a man to dedicate something rashly
    and only later to consider his vows.

26 A wise king winnows out the wicked;
    he drives the threshing wheel over them.

27 The lamp of the Lord searches the spirit of a man *a*;
    it searches out his inmost being.

28 Love and faithfulness keep a king safe;
    through love his throne is made secure.

29 The glory of young men is their strength,
    gray hair the splendor of the old.

30 Blows and wounds cleanse away evil,
    and beatings purge the inmost being.

DAY 21

Psalm 21
For the director of music. A psalm of David.

1 O Lord, the king rejoices in your strength.
    How great is his joy in the victories you give!

2 You have granted him the desire of his heart

---

*a*27 Or *The spirit of man is the Lord's lamp*

and have not withheld the request
of his lips. *Selah*

3 You welcomed him with rich blessings
and placed a crown of pure gold on his head.

4 He asked you for life, and you gave it to him—
length of days, for ever and ever.

5 Through the victories you gave, his glory
is great;
you have bestowed on him splendor and
majesty.

6 Surely you have granted him eternal blessings
and made him glad with the joy of your
presence.

7 For the king trusts in the Lord;
through the unfailing love of the Most High
he will not be shaken.

8 Your hand will lay hold on all your enemies;
your right hand will seize your foes.

9 At the time of your appearing
you will make them like a fiery furnace.
In his wrath the Lord will swallow them up,
and his fire will consume them.

10 You will destroy their descendants from the
earth,
their posterity from mankind.

11 Though they plot evil against you
and devise wicked schemes, they cannot
succeed;

12 for you will make them turn their backs
when you aim at them with drawn bow.

13 Be exalted, O Lord, in your strength;
we will sing and praise your might.

Psalm 51

For the director of music. A psalm of David.
When the prophet Nathan came to him after David
had committed adultery with Bathsheba.

1   Have mercy on me, O God,
        according to your unfailing love;
    according to your great compassion
        blot out my transgressions.
2   Wash away all my iniquity
        and cleanse me from my sin.

3   For I know my transgressions,
        and my sin is always before me.
4   Against you, you only, have I sinned
        and done what is evil in your sight,
    so that you are proved right when you speak
        and justified when you judge.
5   Surely I was sinful at birth,
        sinful from the time my mother conceived me.
6   Surely you desire truth in the inner parts [a];
        you teach [b] me wisdom in the inmost place.

7   Cleanse me with hyssop, and I will be clean;
        wash me, and I will be whiter than snow.
8   Let me hear joy and gladness;
        let the bones you have crushed rejoice.
9   Hide your face from my sins
        and blot out all my iniquity.

10 Create in me a pure heart, O God,
        and renew a steadfast spirit within me.
11 Do not cast me from your presence

---

[a]6 The meaning of the Hebrew for this phrase is uncertain.
[b]6 Or *you desired . . . ; / you taught*

> or take your Holy Spirit from me.
12 Restore to me the joy of your salvation
> and grant me a willing spirit, to sustain me.

13 Then I will teach transgressors your ways,
> and sinners will turn back to you.
14 Save me from bloodguilt, O God,
> the God who saves me,
> and my tongue will sing of your righteousness.
15 O Lord, open my lips,
> and my mouth will declare your praise.
16 You do not delight in sacrifice, or I would bring it;
> you do not take pleasure in burnt offerings.
17 The sacrifices of God are [a] a broken spirit;
> a broken and contrite heart,
> O God, you will not despise.

18 In your good pleasure make Zion prosper;
> build up the walls of Jerusalem.
19 Then there will be righteous sacrifices,
> whole burnt offerings to delight you;
> then bulls will be offered on your altar.

Psalm 81

For the director of music. According to *gittith*. [b]
Of Asaph.

1 Sing for joy to God our strength;
> shout aloud to the God of Jacob!
2 Begin the music, strike the tambourine,
> play the melodious harp and lyre.
3 Sound the ram's horn at the New Moon,

---

[a]17 Or *My sacrifice, O God, is*   [b] Title: Probably a musical term

and when the moon is full, on the day of our
Feast;
4 this is a decree for Israel,
an ordinance of the God of Jacob.
5 He established it as a statute for Joseph
when he went out against Egypt,
where we heard a language we did not
understand. *a*

6 He says, "I removed the burden from their
shoulders;
their hands were set free from the basket.
7 In your distress you called and I rescued you,
I answered you out of a thundercloud;
I tested you at the waters of Meribah.   *Selah*

8 Hear, O my people, and I will warn you—
if you would but listen to me, O Israel!
9 You shall have no foreign god among you;
you shall not bow down to an alien god.
10 I am the Lord your God,
who brought you up out of Egypt.
Open wide your mouth and I will fill it.

11 But my people would not listen to me;
Israel would not submit to me.
12 So I gave them over to their stubborn hearts
to follow their own devices.

13 If my people would but listen to me,
if Israel would follow my ways,
14 how quickly would I subdue their enemies
and turn my hand against their foes!

*a*5 Or / *and we heard a voice we had not known*

15 Those who hate the Lord would cringe before
   him,
   and their punishment would last forever.
16 But you would be fed with the finest of wheat;
   with honey from the rock I would satisfy
   you."

Psalm 111 ^a

1 Praise the Lord. ^b

   I will extol the Lord with all my heart
   in the council of the upright and in the assembly.

2 Great are the works of the Lord;
   they are pondered by all who delight in them.
3 Glorious and majestic are his deeds,
   and his righteousness endures forever.
4 He has caused his wonders to be remembered;
   the Lord is gracious and compassionate.
5 He provides food for those who fear him;
   he remembers his covenant forever.
6 He has shown his people the power of his works,
   giving them the lands of other nations.
7 The works of his hands are faithful and just;
   all his precepts are trustworthy.
8 They are steadfast for ever and ever,
   done in faithfulness and uprightness.
9 He provided redemption for his people;
   he ordained his covenant forever—
   holy and awesome is his name.

---

^a This psalm is an acrostic poem, the lines of which begin with the
successive letters of the Hebrew alphabet.   ^b1 Hebrew *Hallelu Yah*

10   The fear of the Lord is the beginning of wisdom;
    all who follow his precepts have good
      understanding.
    To him belongs eternal praise.

Psalm 141
A psalm of David.

1   O Lord, I call to you; come quickly to me.
    Hear my voice when I call to you.
2   May my prayer be set before you like incense;
    may the lifting up of my hands be like the
      evening sacrifice.

3   Set a guard over my mouth, O Lord;
    keep watch over the door of my lips.
4   Let not my heart be drawn to what is evil,
    to take part in wicked deeds
with men who are evildoers;
    let me not eat of their delicacies.

5   Let a righteous man *a* strike me—it is a kindness;
    let him rebuke me—it is oil on my head.
    My head will not refuse it.

    Yet my prayer is ever against the deeds of evil-
      doers;
6   their rulers will be thrown down from
      the cliffs,
    and the wicked will learn that my words
      were well spoken.
7   They will say, "As one plows and breaks up
      the earth,

a5 Or *Let the Righteous One*

so our bones have been scattered at the mouth
of the grave. [a]"

8   But my eyes are fixed on you, O Sovereign Lord;
in you I take refuge—do not give me over to death.

9   Keep me from the snares they have laid for me,
from the traps set by evildoers.

10 Let the wicked fall into their own nets,
while I pass by in safety.

Proverbs 21

1   The king's heart is in the hand of the Lord;
he directs it like a watercourse wherever he
pleases.

2   All a man's ways seem right to him,
but the Lord weighs the heart.

3   To do what is right and just
is more acceptable to the Lord than sacrifice.

4   Haughty eyes and a proud heart,
the lamp of the wicked, are sin!

5   The plans of the diligent lead to profit
as surely as haste leads to poverty.

6   A fortune made by a lying tongue
is a fleeting vapor and a deadly snare. [b]

7   The violence of the wicked will drag them away,
for they refuse to do what is right.

---

[a]7 Hebrew *Sheol*   [b]6 Some Hebrew manuscripts, Septuagint and
Vulgate; most Hebrew manuscripts *vapor for those who seek death*

8   The way of the guilty is devious,
        but the conduct of the innocent is upright.

9   Better to live on a corner of the roof
        than share a house with a quarrelsome wife.

10 The wicked man craves evil;
        his neighbor gets no mercy from him.

11 When a mocker is punished, the simple gain
            wisdom;
        when a wise man is instructed, he gets
            knowledge.

12 The Righteous One [a] takes note of the house of the
            wicked
        and brings the wicked to ruin.

13 If a man shuts his ears to the cry of the poor,
        he too will cry out and not be answered.

14 A gift given in secret soothes anger,
        and a bribe concealed in the cloak pacifies great
            wrath.

15 When justice is done, it brings joy to the righteous
        but terror to evildoers.

16 A man who strays from the path of understanding
        comes to rest in the company of the dead.

17 He who loves pleasure will become poor;
        whoever loves wine and oil will never be rich.

18 The wicked become a ransom for the righteous,
        and the unfaithful for the upright.

---

[a]12 Or *The righteous man*

19 Better to live in a desert
      than with a quarrelsome and ill-tempered wife.

20 In the house of the wise are stores of choice food
      and oil,
      but a foolish man devours all he has.

21 He who pursues righteousness and love
      finds life, prosperity ^{a} and honor.

22 A wise man attacks the city of the mighty
      and pulls down the stronghold in which they
      trust.

23 He who guards his mouth and his tongue
      keeps himself from calamity.

24 The proud and arrogant man—"Mocker" is his name;
      he behaves with overweening pride.

25 The sluggard's craving will be the death of him,
      because his hands refuse to work.

26 All day long he craves for more,
      but the righteous give without sparing.

27 The sacrifice of the wicked is detestable—
      how much more so when brought with evil
      intent!

28 A false witness will perish,
      and whoever listens to him will be destroyed
      forever. ^{b}

29 A wicked man puts up a bold front,
      but an upright man gives thought to his ways.

^{a}21 Or *righteousness* ^{b}28 Or / *but the words of an obedient man will live on*

30 There is no wisdom, no insight, no plan
      that can succeed against the Lord.

31 The horse is made ready for the day of battle,
      but victory rests with the Lord.

DAY 22

Psalm 22

For the director of music. To the tune of
"The Doe of the Morning." A psalm of David.

1 My God, my God, why have you forsaken me?
      Why are you so far from saving me,
        so far from the words of my groaning?

2 O my God, I cry out by day, but you do not answer,
      by night, and am not silent.

3 Yet you are enthroned as the Holy One;
      you are the praise of Israel. *a*

4 In you our fathers put their trust;
      they trusted and you delivered them.

5 They cried to you and were saved;
      in you they trusted and were not disappointed.

6 But I am a worm and not a man,
      scorned by men and despised by the people.

7 All who see me mock me;
      they hurl insults, shaking their heads:

8 "He trusts in the Lord;
      let the Lord rescue him.
    Let him deliver him,
      since he delights in him."

*a*3 Or *Yet you are holy, / enthroned on the praises of Israel*

9 Yet you brought me out of the womb;
    you made me trust in you
    even at my mother's breast.

10 From birth I was cast upon you;
    from my mother's womb you have been my
        God.

11 Do not be far from me,
    for trouble is near
    and there is no one to help.

12 Many bulls surround me;
    strong bulls of Bashan encircle me.

13 Roaring lions tearing their prey
    open their mouths wide against me.

14 I am poured out like water,
    and all my bones are out of joint.
    My heart has turned to wax;
    it has melted away within me.

15 My strength is dried up like a potsherd,
    and my tongue sticks to the roof of my mouth;
    you lay me *a* in the dust of death.

16 Dogs have surrounded me;
    a band of evil men has encircled me,
    they have pierced *b* my hands and my feet.

17 I can count all my bones;
    people stare and gloat over me.

18 They divide my garments among them
    and cast lots for my clothing.

19 But you, O Lord, be not far off;
    O my Strength, come quickly to help me.

---

*a*15 Or / I am laid   *b*16 Some Hebrew manuscripts, Septuagint and
Syriac; most Hebrew manuscripts / like the lion,

20 Deliver my life from the sword,
my precious life from the power of the dogs.
21 Rescue me from the mouth of the lions;
save *a* me from the horns of the wild oxen.
22 I will declare your name to my brothers;
in the congregation I will praise you.
23 You who fear the Lord, praise him!
All you descendants of Jacob, honor him!
Revere him, all you descendants of Israel!
24 For he has not despised or disdained
the suffering of the afflicted one;
he has not hidden his face from him
but has listened to his cry for help.

25 From you comes the theme of my praise in the
great assembly;
before those who fear you, *b* will I fulfill my
vows.
26 The poor will eat and be satisfied;
they who seek the Lord will praise him—
may your hearts live forever!
27 All the ends of the earth
will remember and turn to the Lord,
and all the families of the nations
will bow down before him,
28 for dominion belongs to the Lord
and he rules over the nations.

29 All the rich of the earth will feast and worship;
all who go down to the dust will kneel before
him—
those who cannot keep themselves alive.
30 Posterity will serve him;

*a*21 Or / *you have heard*   *b*25 Hebrew *him*

> future generations will be told about
> the Lord.

31 They will proclaim his righteousness
    to a people yet unborn—
        for he has done it.

Psalm 52

For the director of music. A *maskil* ^a of David. When
Doeg the Edomite had gone to Saul and told him:
"David has gone to the house of Ahimelech."

1 Why do you boast of evil, you mighty man?
       Why do you boast all day long,
           you who are a disgrace in the eyes of God?
2 Your tongue plots destruction;
       it is like a sharpened razor,
       you who practice deceit.
3 You love evil rather than good,
       falsehood rather than speaking the truth.   *Selah*
4 You love every harmful word,
       O you deceitful tongue!

5 Surely God will bring you down to everlasting
        ruin:
       He will snatch you up and tear you from your
           tent;
       he will uproot you from the land of the
           living.   *Selah*
6 The righteous will see and fear;
       they will laugh at him, saying,
7 "Here now is the man
       who did not make God his stronghold

---

^a Title: Probably a literary or musical term

but trusted in his great wealth
and grew strong by destroying others!"

8 But I am like an olive tree
flourishing in the house of God;
I trust in God's unfailing love
for ever and ever.
9 I will praise you forever for what you have done;
in your name I will hope, for your
name is good.
I will praise you in the presence
of your saints.

Psalm 82

A psalm of Asaph.

1 God presides in the great assembly;
he gives judgment among the "gods":

2 "How long will you *a* defend the unjust
and show partiality to the wicked?   *Selah*
3 Defend the cause of the weak and fatherless;
maintain the rights of the poor and oppressed.
4 Rescue the weak and needy;
deliver them from the hand of the wicked.

5 They know nothing, they understand nothing.
They walk about in darkness;
all the foundations of the earth are shaken.

6 I said, 'You are "gods";
you are all sons of the Most High.'
7 But you will die like mere men;
you will fall like every other ruler."

a2 The Hebrew is plural.

8   Rise up, O God, judge the earth,
         for all the nations are your inheritance.

Psalm 112 ^a

1   Praise the Lord. ^b

     Blessed is the man who fears the Lord,
         who finds great delight in his commands.

2   His children will be mighty in the land;
         the generation of the upright will be blessed.

3   Wealth and riches are in his house,
         and his righteousness endures forever.

4   Even in darkness light dawns for the upright,
         for the gracious and compassionate and
             righteous man. ^c

5   Good will come to him who is generous and lends
             freely,
         who conducts his affairs with justice.

6   Surely he will never be shaken;
         a righteous man will be remembered forever.

7   He will have no fear of bad news;
         his heart is steadfast, trusting in the Lord.

8   His heart is secure, he will have no fear;
         in the end he will look in triumph on his foes.

9   He has scattered abroad his gifts to the poor,
         his righteousness endures forever;
         his horn ^d will be lifted high in honor.

^a This psalm is an acrostic poem, the lines of which begin with the
successive letters of the Hebrew alphabet.   ^b1 Hebrew *Hallelu Yah*
^c4 Or / *for the Lord is gracious and compassionate and righteous*
^d9 *Horn* here symbolizes dignity.

10 The wicked man will see and be vexed,
    he will gnash his teeth and waste away;
    the longings of the wicked will come
      to nothing.

Psalm 142

A *maskil* [a] of David. When he was in the cave.
A prayer.

1 I cry aloud to the Lord;
    I lift up my voice to the Lord for mercy.
2 I pour out my complaint before him;
    before him I tell my trouble.

3 When my spirit grows faint within me,
    it is you who know my way.
    In the path where I walk
      men have hidden a snare for me.
4 Look to my right and see;
    no one is concerned for me.
    I have no refuge;
      no one cares for my life.

5 I cry to you, O Lord;
    I say, "You are my refuge,
      my portion in the land of the living."
6 Listen to my cry,
    for I am in desperate need;
    rescue me from those who pursue me,
      for they are too strong for me.
7 Set me free from my prison,
    that I may praise your name.

_____

[a] Title: Probably a literary or musical term

Then the righteous will gather about me
because of your goodness to me.

Proverbs 22

1   A good name is more desirable than great
riches;
to be esteemed is better than silver or gold.

2   Rich and poor have this in common:
The Lord is the Maker of them all.

3   A prudent man sees danger and takes refuge,
but the simple keep going and suffer for it.

4   Humility and the fear of the Lord
bring wealth and honor and life.

5   In the paths of the wicked lie thorns and snares,
but he who guards his soul stays far from
them.

6   Train *a* a child in the way he should go,
and when he is old he will not turn from it.

7   The rich rule over the poor,
and the borrower is servant to the lender.

8   He who sows wickedness reaps trouble,
and the rod of his fury will be destroyed.

9   A generous man will himself be blessed,
for he shares his food with the poor.

10   Drive out the mocker, and out goes strife;
quarrels and insults are ended.

a6 Or Start

11 He who loves a pure heart and whose speech is
      gracious
    will have the king for his friend.

12 The eyes of the Lord keep watch over knowledge,
    but he frustrates the words of the unfaithful.

13 The sluggard says, "There is a lion outside!"
    or, "I will be murdered in the streets!"

14 The mouth of an adulteress is a deep pit;
    he who is under the Lord's wrath will fall into it.

15 Folly is bound up in the heart of a child,
    but the rod of discipline will drive it far from
      him.

16 He who oppresses the poor to increase his
      wealth
    and he who gives gifts to the rich—both come
      to poverty.

17 Pay attention and listen to the sayings of the wise;
    apply your heart to what I teach,

18 for it is pleasing when you keep them in your
      heart
    and have all of them ready on your lips.

19 So that your trust may be in the Lord,
    I teach you today, even you.

20 Have I not written thirty [a] sayings for you,
    sayings of counsel and knowledge,

21 teaching you true and reliable words,
    so that you can give sound answers
    to him who sent you?

---

[a]20 Or *not formerly written; or not written excellent*

22 Do not exploit the poor because they
    are poor
    and do not crush the needy in court,
23 for the Lord will take up their case
    and will plunder those who plunder them.

24 Do not make friends with a hot-tempered man,
    do not associate with one easily angered,
25 or you may learn his ways
    and get yourself ensnared.

26 Do not be a man who strikes hands in pledge
    or puts up security for debts;
27 if you lack the means to pay,
    your very bed will be snatched from
      under you.

28 Do not move an ancient boundary stone
    set up by your forefathers.

29 Do you see a man skilled in his work?
    He will serve before kings;
    he will not serve before obscure men.

DAY 23

Psalm 23
A psalm of David.

1 The Lord is my shepherd, I shall not be in want.
2   He makes me lie down in green pastures,
he leads me beside quiet waters,
3   he restores my soul.
He guides me in paths of righteousness
    for his name's sake.

4   Even though I walk
        through the valley of the shadow
            of death, [a]
     I will fear no evil,
        for you are with me;
     your rod and your staff,
        they comfort me.

5   You prepare a table before me
        in the presence of my enemies.
     You anoint my head with oil;
        my cup overflows.

6   Surely goodness and love will follow me
        all the days of my life,
     and I will dwell in the house of the Lord
        forever.

Psalm 53

For the director of music. According to *mahalath.* [b]
A *maskil* [c] of David.

1   The fool says in his heart,
        "There is no God."
     They are corrupt, and their ways are vile;
        there is no one who does good.

2   God looks down from heaven
        on the sons of men
     to see if there are any who understand,
        any who seek God.

3   Everyone has turned away,
        they have together become corrupt;

---

[a]4 Or *through the darkest valley*   [b] Title: Probably a musical term
[c] Title: Probably a literary or musical term

there is no one who does good,
not even one.

4 Will the evildoers never learn—
those who devour my people as men eat bread
and who do not call on God?
5 There they were, overwhelmed with dread,
where there was nothing to dread.
God scattered the bones of those who attacked
you;
you put them to shame, for God despised
them.

6 Oh, that salvation for Israel would come out of
Zion!
When God restores the fortunes of his people,
let Jacob rejoice and Israel be glad!

Psalm 83

A song. A psalm of Asaph.

1 O God, do not keep silent;
be not quiet, O God, be not still.
2 See how your enemies are astir,
how your foes rear their heads.
3 With cunning they conspire against your people;
they plot against those you cherish.
4 "Come," they say, "let us destroy them as a nation,
that the name of Israel be remembered no
more."

5 With one mind they plot together;
they form an alliance against you—
6 the tents of Edom and the Ishmaelites,
of Moab and the Hagrites,

7 Gebal, ^a Ammon and Amalek,
   Philistia, with the people of Tyre.
8 Even Assyria has joined them
   to lend strength to the descendants of Lot.   *Selah*

9 Do to them as you did to Midian,
   as you did to Sisera and Jabin at the river Kishon,
10 who perished at Endor
   and became like refuse on the ground.
11 Make their nobles like Oreb and Zeeb,
   all their princes like Zebah and Zalmunna,
12 who said, "Let us take possession
   of the pasturelands of God."

13 Make them like tumbleweed, O my God,
   like chaff before the wind.
14 As fire consumes the forest
   or a flame sets the mountains ablaze,
15 so pursue them with your tempest
   and terrify them with your storm.
16 Cover their faces with shame
   so that men will seek your name, O Lord.

17 May they ever be ashamed and dismayed;
   may they perish in disgrace.
18 Let them know that you, whose name is the Lord—
   that you alone are the Most High over all the
   earth.

Psalm 113

1 Praise the Lord. ^b

   Praise, O servants of the Lord,

---

^a7 That is, Byblos   ^b1 Hebrew *Hallelu Yah*; also in verse 9

praise the name of the Lord.
2 Let the name of the Lord be praised,
       both now and forevermore.
3 From the rising of the sun to the place where it
           sets,
       the name of the Lord is to be praised.

4 The Lord is exalted over all the nations,
       his glory above the heavens.
5 Who is like the Lord our God,
       the One who sits enthroned on high,
6 who stoops down to look
       on the heavens and the earth?

7 He raises the poor from the dust
       and lifts the needy from the ash heap;
8 he seats them with princes,
       with the princes of their people.
9 He settles the barren woman in her home
       as a happy mother of children.

Praise the Lord.

Psalm 143

A psalm of David.

1 O Lord, hear my prayer,
       listen to my cry for mercy;
   in your faithfulness and righteousness
       come to my relief.
2 Do not bring your servant into judgment,
       for no one living is righteous before you.

3 The enemy pursues me,
       he crushes me to the ground;
   he makes me dwell in darkness

    like those long dead.
4 So my spirit grows faint within me;
    my heart within me is dismayed.

5 I remember the days of long ago;
    I meditate on all your works
    and consider what your hands have done.
6 I spread out my hands to you;
    my soul thirsts for you like a
        parched land.   *Selah*

7 Answer me quickly, O Lord;
    my spirit faints with longing.
Do not hide your face from me
    or I will be like those who go down
        to the pit.
8 Let the morning bring me word of your
        unfailing love,
    for I have put my trust in you.
Show me the way I should go,
    for to you I lift up my soul.
9 Rescue me from my enemies, O Lord,
    for I hide myself in you.
10 Teach me to do your will,
    for you are my God;
may your good Spirit
    lead me on level ground.
11 For your name's sake, O Lord,
        preserve my life;
    in your righteousness, bring me
        out of trouble.
12 In your unfailing love, silence my enemies;
    destroy all my foes,
    for I am your servant.

Proverbs 23

1 When you sit to dine with a ruler,
    note well what [a] is before you,
2 and put a knife to your throat
    if you are given to gluttony.
3 Do not crave his delicacies,
    for that food is deceptive.

4 Do not wear yourself out to get rich;
    have the wisdom to show restraint.
5 Cast but a glance at riches, and they are gone,
    for they will surely sprout wings
    and fly off to the sky like an eagle.

6 Do not eat the food of a stingy man,
    do not crave his delicacies;
7 for he is the kind of man
    who is always thinking about the cost. [b]
"Eat and drink," he says to you,
    but his heart is not with you.
8 You will vomit up the little you have eaten
    and will have wasted your compliments.

9 Do not speak to a fool,
    for he will scorn the wisdom of your words.

10 Do not move an ancient boundary stone
    or encroach on the fields of the fatherless,
11 for their Defender is strong;
    he will take up their case against you.

12 Apply your heart to instruction
    and your ears to words of knowledge.

---

[a]1 Or *who*   [b]7 Or *for as he thinks within himself,* / *so he is;* or *for as he puts on a feast,* / *so he is*

13 Do not withhold discipline from a child;
  if you punish him with the rod,
   he will not die.
14 Punish him with the rod
  and save his soul from death. *ᵃ*

15 My son, if your heart is wise,
  then my heart will be glad;
16 my inmost being will rejoice
  when your lips speak what is right.

17 Do not let your heart envy sinners,
  but always be zealous for the fear of the Lord.
18 There is surely a future hope for you,
  and your hope will not be cut off.
19 Listen, my son, and be wise,
  and keep your heart on the right path.
20 Do not join those who drink too much wine
  or gorge themselves on meat,
21 for drunkards and gluttons become poor,
  and drowsiness clothes them in rags.

22 Listen to your father, who gave you life,
  and do not despise your mother when she is old.
23 Buy the truth and do not sell it;
  get wisdom, discipline and understanding.
24 The father of a righteous man has great joy;
  he who has a wise son delights in him.
25 May your father and mother be glad;
  may she who gave you birth rejoice!

26 My son, give me your heart
  and let your eyes keep to my ways,

*ᵃ*14 Hebrew *Sheol*

27   for a prostitute is a deep pit
      and a wayward wife is a narrow well.

28   Like a bandit she lies in wait,
      and multiplies the unfaithful among men.

29   Who has woe? Who has sorrow?
      Who has strife? Who has complaints?
      Who has needless bruises? Who has bloodshot
        eyes?

30   Those who linger over wine,
      who go to sample bowls of mixed wine.

31   Do not gaze at wine when it is red,
      when it sparkles in the cup,
      when it goes down smoothly!

32   In the end it bites like a snake
      and poisons like a viper.

33   Your eyes will see strange sights
      and your mind imagine confusing things.

34   You will be like one sleeping on the high seas,
      lying on top of the rigging.

35   "They hit me," you will say, "but I'm not hurt!
      They beat me, but I don't feel it!
      When will I wake up
        so I can find another drink?"

DAY 24

Psalm 24
Of David. A psalm.

1   The earth is the Lord's, and everything in it,
      the world, and all who live in it;

2   for he founded it upon the seas
      and established it upon the waters.

3 Who may ascend the hill of the Lord?
    Who may stand in his holy place?
4 He who has clean hands and a pure heart,
    who does not lift up his soul to an idol
    or swear by what is false. *a*
5 He will receive blessing from the Lord
    and vindication from God his Savior.
6 Such is the generation of those who seek him,
    who seek your face, O God of Jacob. *b*   *Selah*

7 Lift up your heads, O you gates;
    be lifted up, you ancient doors,
    that the King of glory may come in.
8 Who is this King of glory?
    The Lord strong and mighty,
    the Lord mighty in battle.
9 Lift up your heads, O you gates;
    lift them up, you ancient doors,
    that the King of glory may come in.
10 Who is he, this King of glory?
    The Lord Almighty—
    he is the King of glory.   *Selah*

Psalm 54

For the director of music. With stringed instruments.
A *maskil* *a* of David. When the Ziphites had gone to
Saul and said, "Is not David hiding among us?"

1 Save me, O God, by your name;
    vindicate me by your might.

*a*4 Or *swear falsely*   *b*6 Two Hebrew manuscripts and Syriac (see
also Septuagint); most Hebrew manuscripts *face, Jacob*
c Title: Probably a literary or musical term

2 Hear my prayer, O God;
    listen to the words of my mouth.

3 Strangers are attacking me;
    ruthless men seek my life—
    men without regard for God.   *Selah*

4 Surely God is my help;
    the Lord is the one who sustains me.

5 Let evil recoil on those who slander me;
    in your faithfulness destroy them.

6 I will sacrifice a freewill offering to you;
    I will praise your name, O Lord,
    for it is good.

7 For he has delivered me from all my troubles,
    and my eyes have looked in triumph on my foes.

Psalm 84

For the director of music. According to *gittith*. [a]
Of the Sons of Korah. A psalm.

1 How lovely is your dwelling place,
    O Lord Almighty!

2 My soul yearns, even faints,
    for the courts of the Lord;
    my heart and my flesh cry out
    for the living God.

3 Even the sparrow has found a home,
    and the swallow a nest for herself,
    where she may have her young—
    a place near your altar,

[a] Title: Probably a musical term

O Lord Almighty, my King and my God.

4 Blessed are those who dwell in your house;
they are ever praising you.   *Selah*

5 Blessed are those whose strength is in you,
who have set their hearts on pilgrimage.

6 As they pass through the Valley of Baca,
they make it a place of springs;
the autumn rains also cover it with pools. *ᵃ*

7 They go from strength to strength,
till each appears before God in Zion.

8 Hear my prayer, O Lord God Almighty;
listen to me, O God of Jacob.   *Selah*

9 Look upon our shield, *ᵇ* O God;
look with favor on your anointed one.

10 Better is one day in your courts
than a thousand elsewhere;
I would rather be a doorkeeper in the house
of my God
than dwell in the tents of the wicked.

11 For the Lord God is a sun and shield;
the Lord bestows favor and honor;
no good thing does he withhold
from those whose walk is blameless.

12 O Lord Almighty,
blessed is the man who trusts in you.

Psalm 114

1 When Israel came out of Egypt,
the house of Jacob from a people of foreign tongue,

ᵃ6 Or blessings   ᵇ9 Or sovereign

2 Judah became God's sanctuary,
   Israel his dominion.

3 The sea looked and fled,
   the Jordan turned back;
4 the mountains skipped like rams,
   the hills like lambs.

5 Why was it, O sea, that you fled,
   O Jordan, that you turned back,
6 you mountains, that you skipped like rams,
   you hills, like lambs?

7 Tremble, O earth, at the presence of the Lord,
   at the presence of the God of Jacob,
8 who turned the rock into a pool,
   the hard rock into springs of water.

Psalm 144

Of David.

1 Praise be to the Lord my Rock,
   who trains my hands for war,
   my fingers for battle.
2 He is my loving God and my fortress,
   my stronghold and my deliverer,
   my shield, in whom I take refuge,
   who subdues peoples ^a under me.

3 O Lord, what is man that you care for him,
   the son of man that you think of him?

---

^a2 Many manuscripts of the Masoretic Text, Dead Sea Scrolls, Aquila,
Jerome and Syriac; most manuscripts of the Masoretic Text *subdues my
people*

4 Man is like a breath;
    his days are like a fleeting shadow.
5 Part your heavens, O Lord, and come down;
    touch the mountains, so that they smoke.
6 Send forth lightning and scatter the enemies;
    shoot your arrows and rout them.
7 Reach down your hand from on high;
    deliver me and rescue me
from the mighty waters,
    from the hands of foreigners
8 whose mouths are full of lies,
    whose right hands are deceitful.

9 I will sing a new song to you, O God;
    on the ten-stringed lyre I will make music to you,
10 to the One who gives victory to kings,
    who delivers his servant David from the deadly
        sword.

11 Deliver me and rescue me
    from the hands of foreigners
whose mouths are full of lies,
    whose right hands are deceitful.

12 Then our sons in their youth
    will be like well-nurtured plants,
and our daughters will be like pillars
    carved to adorn a palace.
13 Our barns will be filled
    with every kind of provision.
Our sheep will increase by thousands,
    by tens of thousands in our fields;
14   our oxen will draw heavy loads. [a]

---

[a] 14 Or *our chieftains will be firmly established*

There will be no breaching of walls,
　　no going into captivity,
　　no cry of distress in our streets.

15 Blessed are the people of whom this is true;
　　blessed are the people whose God is the Lord.

Proverbs 24

1 Do not envy wicked men,
　　do not desire their company;
2 for their hearts plot violence,
　　and their lips talk about making trouble.

3 By wisdom a house is built,
　　and through understanding it is established;
4 through knowledge its rooms are filled
　　with rare and beautiful treasures.

5 A wise man has great power,
　　and a man of knowledge increases strength;
6 for waging war you need guidance,
　　and for victory many advisers.

7 Wisdom is too high for a fool;
　　in the assembly at the gate he has nothing to say.

8 He who plots evil
　　will be known as a schemer.
9 The schemes of folly are sin,
　　and men detest a mocker.

10 If you falter in times of trouble,
　　how small is your strength!

11 Rescue those being led away to death;
　　hold back those staggering toward slaughter.

12 If you say, "But we knew nothing about this,"
    does not he who weighs the heart perceive it?
  Does not he who guards your life know it?
    Will he not repay each person according to
      what he has done?

13 Eat honey, my son, for it is good;
    honey from the comb is sweet to your taste.
14 Know also that wisdom is sweet to your soul;
    if you find it, there is a future hope for you,
    and your hope will not be cut off.

15 Do not lie in wait like an outlaw against a
      righteous man's house,
    do not raid his dwelling place;
16 for though a righteous man falls seven times, he
      rises again,
    but the wicked are brought down by calamity.

17 Do not gloat when your enemy falls;
    when he stumbles, do not let your heart rejoice,
18 or the Lord will see and disapprove
    and turn his wrath away from him.

19 Do not fret because of evil men
    or be envious of the wicked,
20 for the evil man has no future hope,
    and the lamp of the wicked will be
      snuffed out.

21 Fear the Lord and the king, my son,
    and do not join with the rebellious,
22 for those two will send sudden destruction upon
      them,
    and who knows what calamities they
      can bring?

23 These also are sayings of the wise:

To show partiality in judging is not good:
24 Whoever says to the guilty, "You are innocent"—
peoples will curse him and nations denounce him.
25 But it will go well with those who convict the
guilty,
and rich blessing will come upon them.

26 An honest answer
is like a kiss on the lips.

27 Finish your outdoor work
and get your fields ready;
after that, build your house.

28 Do not testify against your neighbor without
cause,
or use your lips to deceive.
29 Do not say, "I'll do to him as he has done to me;
I'll pay that man back for what he did."

30 I went past the field of the sluggard,
past the vineyard of the man who lacks
judgment;
31 thorns had come up everywhere,
the ground was covered with weeds,
and the stone wall was in ruins.
32 I applied my heart to what I observed
and learned a lesson from what I saw:
33 A little sleep, a little slumber,
a little folding of the hands to rest—
34 and poverty will come on you like a bandit
and scarcity like an armed man. *a*

*a*34 Or *like a vagrant / and scarcity like a beggar*

DAY 25

Psalm 25 [a]
Of David.

1 To you, O Lord, I lift up my soul;
2   in you I trust, O my God.
   Do not let me be put to shame,
      nor let my enemies triumph over me.
3 No one whose hope is in you
      will ever be put to shame,
   but they will be put to shame
      who are treacherous without excuse.

4 Show me your ways, O Lord,
      teach me your paths;
5 guide me in your truth and teach me,
      for you are God my Savior,
      and my hope is in you all day long.
6 Remember, O Lord, your great mercy
         and love,
      for they are from of old.
7 Remember not the sins of my youth
      and my rebellious ways;
   according to your love remember me,
      for you are good, O Lord.

8 Good and upright is the Lord;
      therefore he instructs sinners in his ways.
9 He guides the humble in what is right
      and teaches them his way.

---

[a] This psalm is an acrostic poem, the verses of which begin with the
successive letters of the Hebrew alphabet.

DAY 25

10 All the ways of the Lord are loving and
        faithful
            for those who keep the demands of his
                covenant.
11 For the sake of your name, O Lord,
        forgive my iniquity, though it is great.
12 Who, then, is the man that fears the Lord?
        He will instruct him in the way chosen
            for him.
13 He will spend his days in prosperity,
        and his descendants will inherit the land.
14 The Lord confides in those who fear him;
        he makes his covenant known to them.
15 My eyes are ever on the Lord,
        for only he will release my feet from
            the snare.

16 Turn to me and be gracious to me,
        for I am lonely and afflicted.
17 The troubles of my heart have multiplied;
        free me from my anguish.
18 Look upon my affliction and my distress
        and take away all my sins.
19 See how my enemies have increased
        and how fiercely they hate me!
20 Guard my life and rescue me;
        let me not be put to shame,
            for I take refuge in you.
21 May integrity and uprightness protect me,
        because my hope is in you.

22 Redeem Israel, O God,
        from all their troubles!

Psalm 55

For the director of music. With stringed instruments.
A *maskil* [a] of David.

1   Listen to my prayer, O God,
        do not ignore my plea;
2   hear me and answer me.
    My thoughts trouble me and I am distraught
3   at the voice of the enemy,
        at the stares of the wicked;
    for they bring down suffering upon me
        and revile me in their anger.

4   My heart is in anguish within me;
        the terrors of death assail me.
5   Fear and trembling have beset me;
        horror has overwhelmed me.
6   I said, "Oh, that I had the wings of a dove!
        I would fly away and be at rest—
7   I would flee far away
        and stay in the desert;   Selah
8   I would hurry to my place of shelter,
        far from the tempest and storm."

9   Confuse the wicked, O Lord, confound their
            speech,
        for I see violence and strife in the city.
10 Day and night they prowl about on its walls;
        malice and abuse are within it.
11 Destructive forces are at work in the city;
        threats and lies never leave its streets.

12 If an enemy were insulting me,
        I could endure it;

[a] Title: Probably a literary or musical term

if a foe were raising himself against me,
    I could hide from him.
13 But it is you, a man like myself,
    my companion, my close friend,
14 with whom I once enjoyed sweet fellowship
    as we walked with the throng at the house of
        God.

15 Let death take my enemies by surprise;
    let them go down alive to the grave, *a*
    for evil finds lodging among them.

16 But I call to God,
    and the Lord saves me.
17 Evening, morning and noon
    I cry out in distress,
    and he hears my voice.
18 He ransoms me unharmed
    from the battle waged against me,
    even though many oppose me.
19 God, who is enthroned forever,
    will hear them and afflict them—   *Selah*
men who never change their ways
    and have no fear of God.

20 My companion attacks his friends;
    he violates his covenant.
21 His speech is smooth as butter,
    yet war is in his heart;
his words are more soothing than oil,
    yet they are drawn swords.
22 Cast your cares on the Lord
    and he will sustain you;

a15 Hebrew *Sheol*

he will never let the righteous fall.
23 But you, O God, will bring down the
    wicked
    into the pit of corruption;
bloodthirsty and deceitful men
    will not live out half their days.

But as for me, I trust in you.

Psalm 85

For the director of music. Of the Sons of Korah.
A psalm.

1 You showed favor to your land, O Lord;
    you restored the fortunes of Jacob.
2 You forgave the iniquity of your people
    and covered all their sins.

Selah

3 You set aside all your wrath
    and turned from your fierce anger.

4 Restore us again, O God our Savior,
    and put away your displeasure toward us.
5 Will you be angry with us forever?
    Will you prolong your anger through all
    generations?
6 Will you not revive us again,
    that your people may rejoice in you?
7 Show us your unfailing love, O Lord,
    and grant us your salvation.

8 I will listen to what God the Lord will say;
    he promises peace to his people,
      his saints—
but let them not return to folly.

9   Surely his salvation is near those who fear him,
      that his glory may dwell in our land.

10 Love and faithfulness meet together;
      righteousness and peace kiss each other.
11 Faithfulness springs forth from the earth,
      and righteousness looks down from heaven.
12 The Lord will indeed give what is good,
      and our land will yield its harvest.
13 Righteousness goes before him
      and prepares the way for his steps.

Psalm 115

1   Not to us, O Lord, not to us
      but to your name be the glory,
      because of your love and faithfulness.

2   Why do the nations say,
      "Where is their God?"
3   Our God is in heaven;
      he does whatever pleases him.
4   But their idols are silver and gold,
      made by the hands of men.
5   They have mouths, but cannot speak,
      eyes, but they cannot see;
6   they have ears, but cannot hear,
      noses, but they cannot smell;
7   they have hands, but cannot feel,
      feet, but they cannot walk;
      nor can they utter a sound with their
         throats.
8   Those who make them will be like them,
      and so will all who trust in them.

9 O house of Israel, trust in the Lord—
    he is their help and shield.
10 O house of Aaron, trust in the Lord—
    he is their help and shield.
11 You who fear him, trust in the Lord—
    he is their help and shield.

12 The Lord remembers us and will bless us:
    He will bless the house of Israel,
    he will bless the house of Aaron,
13 he will bless those who fear the Lord—
    small and great alike.

14 May the Lord make you increase,
    both you and your children.
15 May you be blessed by the Lord,
    the Maker of heaven and earth.

16 The highest heavens belong to the Lord,
    but the earth he has given to man.
17 It is not the dead who praise the Lord,
    those who go down to silence;
18 it is we who extol the Lord,
    both now and forevermore.

Praise the Lord. [a]

Psalm 145 [b]
A psalm of praise. Of David.

1 I will exalt you, my God the King;
    I will praise your name for ever and ever.

---

[a]18 Hebrew *Hallelu Yah*   [b] This psalm is an acrostic poem, the
verses of which (including verse 13b) begin with the successive letters
of the Hebrew alphabet.

2   Every day I will praise you
        and extol your name for ever and ever.

3   Great is the Lord and most worthy of praise;
        his greatness no one can fathom.

4   One generation will commend your works to
            another;
        they will tell of your mighty acts.

5   They will speak of the glorious splendor of your
            majesty,
        and I will meditate on your wonderful
            works. [a]

6   They will tell of the power of your awesome
            works,
        and I will proclaim your great deeds.

7   They will celebrate your abundant goodness
        and joyfully sing of your righteousness.

8   The Lord is gracious and compassionate,
        slow to anger and rich in love.

9   The Lord is good to all;
        he has compassion on all he has made.

10   All you have made will praise you, O Lord;
        your saints will extol you.

11   They will tell of the glory of your kingdom
        and speak of your might,

12   so that all men may know of your mighty acts
        and the glorious splendor of your kingdom.

13   Your kingdom is an everlasting kingdom,
        and your dominion endures through all
            generations.

[a]5 Dead Sea Scrolls and Syriac (see also Septuagint); Masoretic Text
*On the glorious splendor of your majesty / and on your wonderful works I
will meditate*

> The Lord is faithful to all his promises
> and loving toward all he has made. [a]

14 The Lord upholds all those who fall
and lifts up all who are bowed down.

15 The eyes of all look to you,
and you give them their food at the proper time.

16 You open your hand
and satisfy the desires of every living thing.

17 The Lord is righteous in all his ways
and loving toward all he has made.

18 The Lord is near to all who call on him,
to all who call on him in truth.

19 He fulfills the desires of those who fear him;
he hears their cry and saves them.

20 The Lord watches over all who love him,
but all the wicked he will destroy.

21 My mouth will speak in praise of the Lord.
Let every creature praise his holy name
for ever and ever.

Proverbs 25

1 These are more proverbs of Solomon, copied by the men of Hezekiah king of Judah:

2 It is the glory of God to conceal a matter;
to search out a matter is the glory of kings.

3 As the heavens are high and the earth is deep,
so the hearts of kings are unsearchable.

---

[a]13 One manuscript of the Masoretic Text, Dead Sea Scrolls and Syriac (see also Septuagint); most manuscripts of the Masoretic Text do not have the last two lines of verse 13.

4   Remove the dross from the silver,
        and out comes material for *a* the silversmith;
5   remove the wicked from the king's presence,
        and his throne will be established through
            righteousness.

6   Do not exalt yourself in the king's presence,
        and do not claim a place among great men;
7   it is better for him to say to you, "Come up here,"
        than for him to humiliate you before a
            nobleman.
    What you have seen with your eyes
8   do not bring *a* hastily to court,
    for what will you do in the end
        if your neighbor puts you to shame?

9   If you argue your case with a neighbor,
        do not betray another man's confidence,
10 or he who hears it may shame you
        and you will never lose your bad reputation.

11 A word aptly spoken
        is like apples of gold in settings of silver.

12 Like an earring of gold or an ornament of fine gold
        is a wise man's rebuke to a listening ear.

13 Like the coolness of snow at harvest time
        is a trustworthy messenger to those who send
            him;
    he refreshes the spirit of his masters.
14 Like clouds and wind without rain
        is a man who boasts of gifts he does not give.

*a*4 Or *comes a vessel from*   *b*7,8 Or *nobleman / on whom you had set
your eyes. / 8 Do not go*

15 Through patience a ruler can be persuaded,
    and a gentle tongue can break a bone.

16 If you find honey, eat just enough—
    too much of it, and you will vomit.

17 Seldom set foot in your neighbor's house—
    too much of you, and he will hate you.

18 Like a club or a sword or a sharp arrow
    is the man who gives false testimony
       against his neighbor.

19 Like a bad tooth or a lame foot
    is reliance on the unfaithful in times of trouble.

20 Like one who takes away a garment on a cold day,
    or like vinegar poured on soda,
    is one who sings songs to a heavy heart.

21 If your enemy is hungry, give him food to eat;
    if he is thirsty, give him water to drink.

22 In doing this, you will heap burning coals on his
       head,
    and the Lord will reward you.

23 As a north wind brings rain,
    so a sly tongue brings angry looks.

24 Better to live on a corner of the roof
    than share a house with a quarrelsome wife.

25 Like cold water to a weary soul
    is good news from a distant land.

26 Like a muddied spring or a polluted well
    is a righteous man who gives way to the wicked.

27 It is not good to eat too much honey,
    nor is it honorable to seek one's own honor.

28 Like a city whose walls are broken down
        is a man who lacks self-control.

DAY 26

Psalm 26
Of David.

1   Vindicate me, O Lord,
        for I have led a blameless life;
    I have trusted in the Lord
        without wavering.
2   Test me, O Lord, and try me,
        examine my heart and my mind;
3   for your love is ever before me,
        and I walk continually in your truth.
4   I do not sit with deceitful men,
        nor do I consort with hypocrites;
5   I abhor the assembly of evildoers
        and refuse to sit with the wicked.
6   I wash my hands in innocence,
        and go about your altar, O Lord,
7   proclaiming aloud your praise
        and telling of all your wonderful deeds.
8   I love the house where you live, O Lord,
        the place where your glory dwells.

9   Do not take away my soul along with
            sinners,
        my life with bloodthirsty men,
10 in whose hands are wicked schemes,
        whose right hands are full of bribes.
11 But I lead a blameless life;
        redeem me and be merciful to me.

12   My feet stand on level ground;
        in the great assembly I will praise the Lord.

Psalm 56

For the director of music. To the tune of "A Dove on
Distant Oaks." Of David. A *miktam*. *a* When the
Philistines had seized him in Gath.

1   Be merciful to me, O God, for men hotly
            pursue me;
        all day long they press their attack.
2   My slanderers pursue me all day long;
        many are attacking me in their pride.

3   When I am afraid,
        I will trust in you.
4   In God, whose word I praise,
        in God I trust; I will not be afraid.
        What can mortal man do to me?

5   All day long they twist my words;
        they are always plotting to harm me.
6   They conspire, they lurk,
        they watch my steps,
        eager to take my life.

7   On no account let them escape;
        in your anger, O God, bring down
            the nations.
8   Record my lament;
        list my tears on your scroll *b*—
        are they not in your record?

---

a Title: Probably a literary or musical term   *b*8 Or / *put my tears in
your wineskin*

9   Then my enemies will turn back
        when I call for help.
        By this I will know that God is for me.
10 In God, whose word I praise,
        in the Lord, whose word I praise—
11 in God I trust; I will not be afraid.
        What can man do to me?

12 I am under vows to you, O God;
        I will present my thank offerings to you.
13 For you have delivered me *a* from death
        and my feet from stumbling,
    that I may walk before God
        in the light of life. *b*

Psalm 86
A prayer of David.

1   Hear, O Lord, and answer me,
        for I am poor and needy.
2   Guard my life, for I am devoted to you.
        You are my God; save your servant
        who trusts in you.
3   Have mercy on me, O Lord,
        for I call to you all day long.
4   Bring joy to your servant,
        for to you, O Lord,
        I lift up my soul.

5   You are forgiving and good, O Lord,
        abounding in love to all who call to you.
6   Hear my prayer, O Lord;
        listen to my cry for mercy.

*a*13 Or *my soul*   *b*13 Or *the land of the living*

7   In the day of my trouble I will call to you,
        for you will answer me.

8   Among the gods there is none like you,
            O Lord;
        no deeds can compare with yours.

9   All the nations you have made
            will come and worship before you, O Lord;
        they will bring glory to your name.

10 For you are great and do marvelous deeds;
        you alone are God.

11 Teach me your way, O Lord,
        and I will walk in your truth;
        give me an undivided heart,
            that I may fear your name.

12 I will praise you, O Lord my God, with all my
            heart;
        I will glorify your name forever.

13 For great is your love toward me;
        you have delivered me from the depths of the
            grave. *a*

14 The arrogant are attacking me, O God;
            a band of ruthless men seeks my life—
        men without regard for you.

15 But you, O Lord, are a compassionate and
            gracious God,
        slow to anger, abounding in love and
            faithfulness.

16 Turn to me and have mercy on me;
        grant your strength to your servant
        and save the son of your maidservant. *b*

---

*a*13 Hebrew *Sheol*   *b*16 Or *save your faithful son*

17   Give me a sign of your goodness,
        that my enemies may see it and be put to shame,
        for you, O Lord, have helped me and comforted
        me.

Psalm 116

1   I love the Lord, for he heard my voice;
        he heard my cry for mercy.

2   Because he turned his ear to me,
        I will call on him as long as I live.

3   The cords of death entangled me,
        the anguish of the grave *a* came upon me;
        I was overcome by trouble and sorrow.

4   Then I called on the name of the Lord:
        "O Lord, save me!"

5   The Lord is gracious and righteous;
        our God is full of compassion.

6   The Lord protects the simplehearted;
        when I was in great need, he saved me.

7   Be at rest once more, O my soul,
        for the Lord has been good to you.

8   For you, O Lord, have delivered my soul from
            death,
        my eyes from tears,
        my feet from stumbling,

9   that I may walk before the Lord
        in the land of the living.

10   I believed; therefore *b* I said,
        "I am greatly afflicted."

*a*3 Hebrew *Sheol*   *b*10 Or *believed even when*

11 And in my dismay I said,
   "All men are liars."

12 How can I repay the Lord
   for all his goodness to me?
13 I will lift up the cup of salvation
   and call on the name of the Lord.
14 I will fulfill my vows to the Lord
   in the presence of all his people.

15 Precious in the sight of the Lord
   is the death of his saints.
16 O Lord, truly I am your servant;
   I am your servant, the son of your
      maidservant ^a;
   you have freed me from my chains.

17 I will sacrifice a thank offering to you
   and call on the name of the Lord.
18 I will fulfill my vows to the Lord
   in the presence of all his people,
19 in the courts of the house of the Lord—
   in your midst, O Jerusalem.

   Praise the Lord. ^b

Psalm 146

1 Praise the Lord. ^c

   Praise the Lord, O my soul.
2   I will praise the Lord all my life;
     I will sing praise to my God as long as I live.

---

^a16 Or *servant, your faithful son*   ^b19 Hebrew *Hallelu Yah*
^c1 Hebrew *Hallelu Yah*; also in verse 10

3 Do not put your trust in princes,
   in mortal men, who cannot save.
4 When their spirit departs, they return to the
   ground;
   on that very day their plans come to nothing.

5 Blessed is he whose help is the God of Jacob,
   whose hope is in the Lord his God,
6 the Maker of heaven and earth,
   the sea, and everything in them—
   the Lord, who remains faithful forever.
7 He upholds the cause of the oppressed
   and gives food to the hungry.
   The Lord sets prisoners free,
8   the Lord gives sight to the blind,
   the Lord lifts up those who are bowed down,
   the Lord loves the righteous.
9 The Lord watches over the alien
   and sustains the fatherless and the widow,
   but he frustrates the ways of the wicked.

10 The Lord reigns forever,
   your God, O Zion, for all generations.

   Praise the Lord.

Proverbs 26

1 Like snow in summer or rain in harvest,
   honor is not fitting for a fool.

2 Like a fluttering sparrow or a darting swallow,
   an undeserved curse does not come to rest.

3 A whip for the horse, a halter for the donkey,
   and a rod for the backs of fools!

4 Do not answer a fool according to his folly,
    or you will be like him yourself.

5 Answer a fool according to his folly,
    or he will be wise in his own eyes.

6 Like cutting off one's feet or drinking violence
    is the sending of a message by the hand of a
        fool.

7 Like a lame man's legs that hang limp
    is a proverb in the mouth of a fool.

8 Like tying a stone in a sling
    is the giving of honor to a fool.

9 Like a thornbush in a drunkard's hand
    is a proverb in the mouth of a fool.

10 Like an archer who wounds at random
    is he who hires a fool or any passer-by.

11 As a dog returns to its vomit,
    so a fool repeats his folly.

12 Do you see a man wise in his own eyes?
    There is more hope for a fool than for him.

13 The sluggard says, "There is a lion in the road,
    a fierce lion roaming the streets!"

14 As a door turns on its hinges,
    so a sluggard turns on his bed.

15 The sluggard buries his hand in the dish;
    he is too lazy to bring it back to his mouth.

16 The sluggard is wiser in his own eyes
    than seven men who answer discreetly.

17 Like one who seizes a dog by the ears
    is a passer-by who meddles in a quarrel not his
    own.

18 Like a madman shooting
    firebrands or deadly arrows
19 is a man who deceives his neighbor
    and says, "I was only joking!"

20 Without wood a fire goes out;
    without gossip a quarrel dies down.

21 As charcoal to embers and as wood to fire,
    so is a quarrelsome man for kindling strife.

22 The words of a gossip are like choice morsels;
    they go down to a man's inmost parts.

23 Like a coating of glaze *a* over earthenware
    are fervent lips with an evil heart.

24 A malicious man disguises himself with his lips,
    but in his heart he harbors deceit.
25 Though his speech is charming, do not believe
    him,
    for seven abominations fill his heart.
26 His malice may be concealed by deception,
    but his wickedness will be exposed in the
    assembly.

27 If a man digs a pit, he will fall into it;
    if a man rolls a stone, it will roll back on him.

28 A lying tongue hates those it hurts,
    and a flattering mouth works ruin.

*a*23 With a different word division of the Hebrew; Masoretic Text *of silver dross*

DAY 27

Psalm 27
Of David.

1   The Lord is my light and my salvation—
        whom shall I fear?
    The Lord is the stronghold of my life—
        of whom shall I be afraid?
2   When evil men advance against me
        to devour my flesh, [a]
    when my enemies and my foes attack me,
        they will stumble and fall.
3   Though an army besiege me,
        my heart will not fear;
    though war break out against me,
        even then will I be confident.

4   One thing I ask of the Lord,
        this is what I seek:
    that I may dwell in the house of the Lord
        all the days of my life,
    to gaze upon the beauty of the Lord
        and to seek him in his temple.
5   For in the day of trouble
        he will keep me safe in his dwelling;
    he will hide me in the shelter of his
            tabernacle
        and set me high upon a rock.
6   Then my head will be exalted
        above the enemies who surround me;

---

[a]2 Or *to slander me*

at his tabernacle will I sacrifice with
   shouts of joy;
  I will sing and make music to the Lord.
7 Hear my voice when I call, O Lord;
   be merciful to me and answer me.
8 My heart says of you, "Seek his *a* face!"
   Your face, Lord, I will seek.
9 Do not hide your face from me,
   do not turn your servant away in anger;
   you have been my helper.
  Do not reject me or forsake me,
   O God my Savior.
10 Though my father and mother forsake
    me,
   the Lord will receive me.
11 Teach me your way, O Lord;
   lead me in a straight path
   because of my oppressors.
12 Do not turn me over to the desire
    of my foes,
   for false witnesses rise up against me,
   breathing out violence.

13 I am still confident of this:
   I will see the goodness of the Lord
   in the land of the living.
14 Wait for the Lord;
   be strong and take heart
   and wait for the Lord.

---

*a*8 Or *To you, O my heart, he has said, "Seek my*

Psalm 57

For the director of music. To the tune of
"Do Not Destroy." Of David. A *miktam.* ^a
When he had fled from Saul into the cave.

1   Have mercy on me, O God, have mercy on me,
        for in you my soul takes refuge.
    I will take refuge in the shadow of your wings
        until the disaster has passed.

2   I cry out to God Most High,
        to God, who fulfills his purpose for me.
3   He sends from heaven and saves me,
        rebuking those who hotly pursue me;   *Selah*
    God sends his love and his faithfulness.

4   I am in the midst of lions;
        I lie among ravenous beasts—
    men whose teeth are spears and arrows,
        whose tongues are sharp swords.

5   Be exalted, O God, above the heavens;
        let your glory be over all the earth.

6   They spread a net for my feet—
        I was bowed down in distress.
    They dug a pit in my path—
        but they have fallen into it themselves.   *Selah*

7   My heart is steadfast, O God,
        my heart is steadfast;
        I will sing and make music.
8   Awake, my soul!
        Awake, harp and lyre!
        I will awaken the dawn.

---

^a Title: Probably a literary or musical term

9   I will praise you, O Lord, among the nations;
         I will sing of you among the peoples.
10   For great is your love, reaching to the heavens;
         your faithfulness reaches to the skies.

11   Be exalted, O God, above the heavens;
         let your glory be over all the earth.

Psalm 87

Of the Sons of Korah. A psalm. A song.

1   He has set his foundation on the holy
                    mountain;
2   the Lord loves the gates of Zion
         more than all the dwellings of Jacob.
3   Glorious things are said of you,
         O city of God: *Selah*
4   "I will record Rahab *a* and Babylon
         among those who acknowledge me—
     Philistia too, and Tyre, along with Cush *b*—
         and will say, 'This *c* one was born in Zion.' "

5   Indeed, of Zion it will be said,
         "This one and that one were born in her,
         and the Most High himself will establish
                    her."
6   The Lord will write in the register of the
                    peoples:
         "This one was born in Zion."   *Selah*
7   As they make music they will sing,
         "All my fountains are in you."

---

*a*4 A poetic name for Egypt   *b*4 That is, the upper Nile region
*c*4 Or "O Rahab and Babylon, / Philistia, Tyre and Cush, / I will record
concerning those who acknowledge me: / 'This

Psalm 117

1 Praise the Lord, all you nations;
    extol him, all you peoples.
2 For great is his love toward us,
    and the faithfulness of the Lord endures forever.

Praise the Lord. ^{a}

Psalm 147

1 Praise the Lord. ^{b}

How good it is to sing praises to our God,
    how pleasant and fitting to praise him!
2 The Lord builds up Jerusalem;
    he gathers the exiles of Israel.
3 He heals the brokenhearted
    and binds up their wounds.

4 He determines the number of the stars
    and calls them each by name.
5 Great is our Lord and mighty in power;
    his understanding has no limit.
6 The Lord sustains the humble
    but casts the wicked to the ground.

7 Sing to the Lord with thanksgiving;
    make music to our God on the harp.
8 He covers the sky with clouds;
    he supplies the earth with rain
    and makes grass grow on the hills.
9 He provides food for the cattle
    and for the young ravens when they call.

^{a}2 Hebrew *Hallelu Yah* ^{b}1 Hebrew *Hallelu Yah*; also in verse 20

¹⁰ His pleasure is not in the strength of the horse,
    nor his delight in the legs of a man;
¹¹ the Lord delights in those who fear him,
    who put their hope in his unfailing love.

¹² Extol the Lord, O Jerusalem;
    praise your God, O Zion,
¹³ for he strengthens the bars of your gates
    and blesses your people within you.
¹⁴ He grants peace to your borders
    and satisfies you with the finest of wheat.

¹⁵ He sends his command to the earth;
    his word runs swiftly.
¹⁶ He spreads the snow like wool
    and scatters the frost like ashes.
¹⁷ He hurls down his hail like pebbles.
    Who can withstand his icy blast?
¹⁸ He sends his word and melts them;
    he stirs up his breezes, and the waters flow.

¹⁹ He has revealed his word to Jacob,
    his laws and decrees to Israel.
²⁰ He has done this for no other nation;
    they do not know his laws.

Praise the Lord.

Proverbs 27

¹ Do not boast about tomorrow,
    for you do not know what a day may bring
        forth.

² Let another praise you, and not your own mouth;
    someone else, and not your own lips.

3 Stone is heavy and sand a burden,
   but provocation by a fool is heavier than both.

4 Anger is cruel and fury overwhelming,
   but who can stand before jealousy?

5 Better is open rebuke
   than hidden love.

6 Wounds from a friend can be trusted,
   but an enemy multiplies kisses.

7 He who is full loathes honey,
   but to the hungry even what is bitter tastes sweet.

8 Like a bird that strays from its nest
   is a man who strays from his home.

9 Perfume and incense bring joy to the heart,
   and the pleasantness of one's friend springs
      from his earnest counsel.

10 Do not forsake your friend and the friend of your
      father,
   and do not go to your brother's house when
      disaster strikes you—
   better a neighbor nearby than a brother far away.

11 Be wise, my son, and bring joy to my heart;
   then I can answer anyone who treats me with
      contempt.

12 The prudent see danger and take refuge,
   but the simple keep going and suffer for it.

13 Take the garment of one who puts up security for
      a stranger;
   hold it in pledge if he does it for a wayward
      woman.

14 If a man loudly blesses his neighbor early in the
        morning,
      it will be taken as a curse.

15 A quarrelsome wife is like
      a constant dripping on a rainy day;
16 restraining her is like restraining the wind
      or grasping oil with the hand.

17 As iron sharpens iron,
      so one man sharpens another.

18 He who tends a fig tree will eat its fruit,
      and he who looks after his master will be honored.

19 As water reflects a face,
      so a man's heart reflects the man.

20 Death and Destruction [a] are never satisfied,
      and neither are the eyes of man.

21 The crucible for silver and the furnace for gold,
      but man is tested by the praise he receives.

22 Though you grind a fool in a mortar,
      grinding him like grain with a pestle,
      you will not remove his folly from him.

23 Be sure you know the condition of your flocks,
      give careful attention to your herds;
24 for riches do not endure forever,
      and a crown is not secure for all generations.
25 When the hay is removed and new growth appears
      and the grass from the hills is gathered in,
26 the lambs will provide you with clothing,
      and the goats with the price of a field.

[a]20 Hebrew *Sheol* and *Abaddon*

27 You will have plenty of goats' milk
        to feed you and your family
        and to nourish your servant girls.

DAY 28

Psalm 28
Of David.

1 To you I call, O Lord my Rock;
        do not turn a deaf ear to me.
    For if you remain silent,
        I will be like those who have gone down
            to the pit.
2 Hear my cry for mercy
        as I call to you for help,
    as I lift up my hands
        toward your Most Holy Place.

3 Do not drag me away with the wicked,
        with those who do evil,
    who speak cordially with their neighbors
        but harbor malice in their hearts.
4 Repay them for their deeds
        and for their evil work;
    repay them for what their hands have done
        and bring back upon them what they
            deserve.
5 Since they show no regard for the works
            of the Lord
        and what his hands have done,
    he will tear them down
        and never build them up again.
6 Praise be to the Lord,

for he has heard my cry for mercy.

7   The Lord is my strength and my shield;
      my heart trusts in him, and I am helped.
    My heart leaps for joy
      and I will give thanks to him in song.

8   The Lord is the strength of his people,
      a fortress of salvation for his anointed one.
9   Save your people and bless your inheritance;
      be their shepherd and carry them forever.

Psalm 58

For the director of music. To the tune of
"Do Not Destroy." Of David. A *miktam*. *a*

1   Do you rulers indeed speak justly?
      Do you judge uprightly among men?
2   No, in your heart you devise injustice,
      and your hands mete out violence on the
         earth.
3   Even from birth the wicked go astray;
      from the womb they are wayward and speak
         lies.
4   Their venom is like the venom of a snake,
      like that of a cobra that has stopped its ears,
5   that will not heed the tune of the charmer,
      however skillful the enchanter may be.

6   Break the teeth in their mouths, O God;
      tear out, O Lord, the fangs of the lions!
7   Let them vanish like water that flows away;
      when they draw the bow, let their arrows be
         blunted.

---

a Title: Probably a literary or musical term

8   Like a slug melting away as it moves along,
       like a stillborn child, may they not see the sun.

9   Before your pots can feel the heat of the thorns—
       whether they be green or dry—
         the wicked will be swept away. *a*

10   The righteous will be glad when they are
       avenged,
       when they bathe their feet in the blood
         of the wicked.

11   Then men will say,
       "Surely the righteous still are rewarded;
       surely there is a God who judges the earth."

Psalm 88

A song. A psalm of the Sons of Korah. For the director
of music. According to *mahalath leannoth.* *b*
A *maskil* *c* of Heman the Ezrahite.

1   O Lord, the God who saves me,
       day and night I cry out before you.

2   May my prayer come before you;
       turn your ear to my cry.

3   For my soul is full of trouble
       and my life draws near the grave. *d*

4   I am counted among those who go down
       to the pit;
       I am like a man without strength.

5   I am set apart with the dead,
       like the slain who lie in the grave,

a9 The meaning of the Hebrew for this verse is uncertain.
b Title: Possibly a tune, "The Suffering of Affliction"
c Title: Probably a literary or musical term   d3 Hebrew Sheol

whom you remember no more,
who are cut off from your care.

6 You have put me in the lowest pit,
in the darkest depths.
7 Your wrath lies heavily upon me;
you have overwhelmed me with all
your waves.   *Selah*
8 You have taken from me my closest friends
and have made me repulsive to them.
I am confined and cannot escape;
9   my eyes are dim with grief.

I call to you, O Lord, every day;
I spread out my hands to you.
10 Do you show your wonders to the dead?
Do those who are dead rise up and
praise you?   *Selah*
11 Is your love declared in the grave,
your faithfulness in Destruction *a*?
12 Are your wonders known in the place
of darkness,
or your righteous deeds in the land
of oblivion?

13 But I cry to you for help, O Lord;
in the morning my prayer comes before you.
14 Why, O Lord, do you reject me
and hide your face from me?

15 From my youth I have been afflicted and close
to death;
I have suffered your terrors and am in despair.
16 Your wrath has swept over me;

*a*11 Hebrew *Abaddon*

your terrors have destroyed me.
17 All day long they surround me like a flood;
   they have completely engulfed me.
18 You have taken my companions and loved ones
       from me;
   the darkness is my closest friend.

Psalm 118

1 Give thanks to the Lord, for he is good;
   his love endures forever.

2 Let Israel say:
   "His love endures forever."
3 Let the house of Aaron say:
   "His love endures forever."
4 Let those who fear the Lord say:
   "His love endures forever."

5 In my anguish I cried to the Lord,
   and he answered by setting me free.
6 The Lord is with me; I will not be afraid.
   What can man do to me?
7 The Lord is with me; he is my helper.
   I will look in triumph on my enemies.

8 It is better to take refuge in the Lord
   than to trust in man.
9 It is better to take refuge in the Lord
   than to trust in princes.

10 All the nations surrounded me,
   but in the name of the Lord I cut them off.
11 They surrounded me on every side,
   but in the name of the Lord I cut them off.
12 They swarmed around me like bees,

but they died out as quickly as burning thorns;
in the name of the Lord I cut them off.
13 I was pushed back and about to fall,
but the Lord helped me.
14 The Lord is my strength and my song;
he has become my salvation.

15 Shouts of joy and victory
resound in the tents of the righteous:
"The Lord's right hand has done mighty
things!
16 The Lord's right hand is lifted high;
the Lord's right hand has done mighty
things!"

17 I will not die but live,
and will proclaim what the Lord has done.
18 The Lord has chastened me severely,
but he has not given me over to death.

19 Open for me the gates of righteousness;
I will enter and give thanks to the Lord.
20 This is the gate of the Lord
through which the righteous may enter.
21 I will give you thanks, for you answered me;
you have become my salvation.

22 The stone the builders rejected
has become the capstone;
23 the Lord has done this,
and it is marvelous in our eyes.
24 This is the day the Lord has made;
let us rejoice and be glad in it.

25 O Lord, save us;
O Lord, grant us success.

26   Blessed is he who comes in the name of
       the Lord.
    From the house of the Lord we bless you. *a*

27   The Lord is God,
    and he has made his light shine upon us.
    With boughs in hand, join in the festal procession
      up *b* to the horns of the altar.

28   You are my God, and I will give you thanks;
    you are my God, and I will exalt you.

29   Give thanks to the Lord, for he is good;
    his love endures forever.

Psalm 148

1   Praise the Lord. *c*

    Praise the Lord from the heavens,
      praise him in the heights above.
2   Praise him, all his angels,
    praise him, all his heavenly hosts.
3   Praise him, sun and moon,
    praise him, all you shining stars.
4   Praise him, you highest heavens
    and you waters above the skies.
5   Let them praise the name of the Lord,
    for he commanded and they were created.
6   He set them in place for ever and ever;
    he gave a decree that will never pass away.

7   Praise the Lord from the earth,
    you great sea creatures and all ocean depths,

---

a26 The Hebrew is plural.   *b27* Or *Bind the festal sacrifice with ropes /
and take it*   *c1* Hebrew *Hallelu Yah; also in verse 14*

8   lightning and hail, snow and clouds,
         stormy winds that do his bidding,
9   you mountains and all hills,
         fruit trees and all cedars,
10   wild animals and all cattle,
         small creatures and flying birds,
11   kings of the earth and all nations,
         you princes and all rulers on earth,
12   young men and maidens,
         old men and children.

13   Let them praise the name of the Lord,
         for his name alone is exalted;
         his splendor is above the earth and
             the heavens.
14   He has raised up for his people a horn, [a]
         the praise of all his saints, of Israel,
         the people close to his heart.

     Praise the Lord.

Proverbs 28

1   The wicked man flees though no one pursues,
         but the righteous are as bold as a lion.

2   When a country is rebellious, it has many rulers,
         but a man of understanding and knowledge
             maintains order.

3   A ruler [b] who oppresses the poor
         is like a driving rain that leaves no crops.

[a]14 *Horn* here symbolizes strong one, that is, king.
[b]3 Or *A poor man*

4 Those who forsake the law praise the wicked,
    but those who keep the law resist them.

5 Evil men do not understand justice,
    but those who seek the Lord understand it fully.

6 Better a poor man whose walk is blameless
    than a rich man whose ways are perverse.

7 He who keeps the law is a discerning son,
    but a companion of gluttons disgraces his father.

8 He who increases his wealth by exorbitant interest
    amasses it for another, who will be kind to the
      poor.

9 If anyone turns a deaf ear to the law,
    even his prayers are detestable.

10 He who leads the upright along an evil path
    will fall into his own trap,
    but the blameless will receive a good
      inheritance.

11 A rich man may be wise in his own eyes,
    but a poor man who has discernment sees
      through him.

12 When the righteous triumph, there is great elation;
    but when the wicked rise to power, men go into
      hiding.

13 He who conceals his sins does not prosper,
    but whoever confesses and renounces them
      finds mercy.

14 Blessed is the man who always fears the Lord,
    but he who hardens his heart falls into trouble.

15 Like a roaring lion or a charging bear
   is a wicked man ruling over a helpless people.

16 A tyrannical ruler lacks judgment,
   but he who hates ill-gotten gain will enjoy a
     long life.

17 A man tormented by the guilt of murder
   will be a fugitive till death;
   let no one support him.

18 He whose walk is blameless is kept safe,
   but he whose ways are perverse will suddenly
     fall.

19 He who works his land will have abundant food,
   but the one who chases fantasies will have his
     fill of poverty.

20 A faithful man will be richly blessed,
   but one eager to get rich will not go
     unpunished.

21 To show partiality is not good—
   yet a man will do wrong for a piece of bread.

22 A stingy man is eager to get rich
   and is unaware that poverty awaits him.

23 He who rebukes a man will in the end gain more
     favor
   than he who has a flattering tongue.

24 He who robs his father or mother
   and says, "It's not wrong"—
   he is partner to him who destroys.

25 A greedy man stirs up dissension,
   but he who trusts in the Lord will prosper.

26   He who trusts in himself is a fool,
         but he who walks in wisdom is kept safe.

27   He who gives to the poor will lack nothing,
         but he who closes his eyes to them receives
            many curses.

28   When the wicked rise to power, people go into
            hiding;
         but when the wicked perish, the righteous
            thrive.

DAY 29

Psalm 29
A psalm of David.

1   Ascribe to the Lord, O mighty ones,
         ascribe to the Lord glory and strength.

2   Ascribe to the Lord the glory due his name;
         worship the Lord in the splendor of his *a*
            holiness.

3   The voice of the Lord is over the waters;
         the God of glory thunders,
         the Lord thunders over the mighty waters.

4   The voice of the Lord is powerful;
         the voice of the Lord is majestic.

5   The voice of the Lord breaks the cedars;
         the Lord breaks in pieces the cedars
            of Lebanon.

6   He makes Lebanon skip like a calf,
         Sirion *b* like a young wild ox.

---

*a*2 Or *Lord with the splendor of*   *b*6 That is, Mount Hermon

7   The voice of the Lord strikes
        with flashes of lightning.
8   The voice of the Lord shakes the desert;
        the Lord shakes the Desert of Kadesh.
9   The voice of the Lord twists the oaks *a*
        and strips the forests bare.
     And in his temple all cry, "Glory!"

10   The Lord sits *b* enthroned over the flood;
        the Lord is enthroned as King forever.
11   The Lord gives strength to his people;
        the Lord blesses his people with peace.

Psalm 59

For the director of music. To the tune of "Do Not
Destroy." Of David. A *miktam*. *c* When Saul had sent
men to watch David's house in order to kill him.

1   Deliver me from my enemies, O God;
        protect me from those who rise up
            against me.
2   Deliver me from evildoers
        and save me from bloodthirsty men.

3   See how they lie in wait for me!
        Fierce men conspire against me
        for no offense or sin of mine, O Lord.
4   I have done no wrong, yet they are ready
            to attack me.
     Arise to help me; look on my plight!
5   O Lord God Almighty, the God of Israel,

---

*a*9 Or *Lord makes the deer give birth*   *b*10 Or *sat*   *c* Title: Probably a
literary or musical term

rouse yourself to punish all the nations;
show no mercy to wicked traitors. *Selah*

6 They return at evening,
snarling like dogs,
and prowl about the city.

7 See what they spew from their mouths—
they spew out swords from their lips,
and they say, "Who can hear us?"

8 But you, O Lord, laugh at them;
you scoff at all those nations.

9 O my Strength, I watch for you;
you, O God, are my fortress, 10 my loving God.
God will go before me
and will let me gloat over those who
slander me.

11 But do not kill them, O Lord our shield, *a*
or my people will forget.
In your might make them wander about,
and bring them down.

12 For the sins of their mouths,
for the words of their lips,
let them be caught in their pride.
For the curses and lies they utter,

13 consume them in wrath,
consume them till they are no more.
Then it will be known to the ends of
the earth
that God rules over Jacob. *Selah*

14 They return at evening,
snarling like dogs,

*a*11 Or *sovereign*

and prowl about the city.
15 They wander about for food
    and howl if not satisfied.
16 But I will sing of your strength,
        in the morning I will sing of your love;
    for you are my fortress,
        my refuge in times of trouble.

17 O my Strength, I sing praise to you;
        you, O God, are my fortress,
        my loving God.

Psalm 89
A *maskil* [a] of Ethan the Ezrahite.

1 I will sing of the Lord's great love forever;
        with my mouth I will make your faithfulness
        known through all generations.
2 I will declare that your love stands firm forever,
        that you established your faithfulness in
        heaven itself.

3 You said, "I have made a covenant with my
        chosen one,
    I have sworn to David my servant,
4 'I will establish your line forever
    and make your throne firm through
        all generations.'"   *Selah*

5 The heavens praise your wonders, O Lord,
        your faithfulness too, in the assembly of the
        holy ones.

---

[a] Title: Probably a literary or musical term

6 For who in the skies above can compare with the
    Lord?
        Who is like the Lord among the heavenly beings?
7 In the council of the holy ones God is greatly
    feared;
        he is more awesome than all who surround him.
8 O Lord God Almighty, who is like you?
        You are mighty, O Lord, and your faithfulness
        surrounds you.

9 You rule over the surging sea;
        when its waves mount up, you still them.
10 You crushed Rahab like one of the slain;
        with your strong arm you scattered your
        enemies.
11 The heavens are yours, and yours also the earth;
        you founded the world and all that is in it.
12 You created the north and the south;
        Tabor and Hermon sing for joy at your name.
13 Your arm is endued with power;
        your hand is strong, your right hand exalted.

14 Righteousness and justice are the foundation of
    your throne;
        love and faithfulness go before you.
15 Blessed are those who have learned to acclaim you,
        who walk in the light of your presence, O Lord.
16 They rejoice in your name all day long;
        they exult in your righteousness.
17 For you are their glory and strength,
        and by your favor you exalt our horn. *a*
18 Indeed, our shield *b* belongs to the Lord,
        our king to the Holy One of Israel.

*a*17 *Horn* here symbolizes strong one.   *b*18 Or *sov*

19 Once you spoke in a vision,
   to your faithful people you said:
   "I have bestowed strength on a warrior;
      I have exalted a young man from among
         the people.
20 I have found David my servant;
      with my sacred oil I have anointed him.
21 My hand will sustain him;
      surely my arm will strengthen him.
22 No enemy will subject him to tribute;
      no wicked man will oppress him.
23 I will crush his foes before him
      and strike down his adversaries.
24 My faithful love will be with him,
      and through my name his horn *a* will
         be exalted.
25 I will set his hand over the sea,
      his right hand over the rivers.
26 He will call out to me, 'You are my Father,
      my God, the Rock my Savior.'
27 I will also appoint him my firstborn,
      the most exalted of the kings of the earth.
28 I will maintain my love to him forever,
      and my covenant with him will never fail.
29 I will establish his line forever,
      his throne as long as the heavens endure.

30 If his sons forsake my law
   and do not follow my statutes,
   violate my decrees
   to keep my commands,
   their sin with the rod,

their iniquity with flogging;
33 but I will not take my love from him,
 nor will I ever betray my faithfulness.
34 I will not violate my covenant
 or alter what my lips have uttered.
35 Once for all, I have sworn by my holiness—
 and I will not lie to David—
36 that his line will continue forever
 and his throne endure before me like the sun;
37 it will be established forever like the moon,
 the faithful witness in the sky."   *Selah*

38 But you have rejected, you have spurned,
 you have been very angry with your anointed
 one.
39 You have renounced the covenant with your
 servant
 and have defiled his crown in the dust.
40 You have broken through all his walls
 and reduced his strongholds to ruins.
41 All who pass by have plundered him;
 he has become the scorn of his neighbors.
42 You have exalted the right hand of his foes;
 you have made all his enemies rejoice.
43 You have turned back the edge of his sword
 and have not supported him in battle.
44 You have put an end to his splendor
 and cast his throne to the ground.
45 You have cut short the days of his youth;
 you have covered him with a mantle
 of shame.   *Selah*

46 How long, O Lord? Will you hide yourself
 forever?
 How long will your wrath burn like fire?

47   Remember how fleeting is my life.
         For what futility you have created all men!
48   What man can live and not see death,
         or save himself from the power of the
             grave ^a?   *Selah*
49   O Lord, where is your former great love,
         which in your faithfulness you swore
             to David?
50   Remember, Lord, how your servant has ^b been
         mocked,
         how I bear in my heart the taunts of all the
             nations,
51   the taunts with which your enemies have
         mocked, O Lord,
         with which they have mocked every step of
             your anointed one.

52   Praise be to the Lord forever!
         Amen and Amen.

Psalm 119 ^c

1   Blessed are they whose ways are blameless,
        who walk according to the law of the Lord.
2   Blessed are they who keep his statutes
        and seek him with all their heart.
3   They do nothing wrong;
        they walk in his ways.
4   You have laid down precepts
        that are to be fully obeyed.

a48 Hebrew *Sheol*   *b50* Or *your servants have*   *c* This psalm is an
acrostic poem; the verses of each stanza begin with the same letter of
the Hebrew alphabet.

5 Oh, that my ways were steadfast
    in obeying your decrees!
6 Then I would not be put to shame
    when I consider all your commands.
7 I will praise you with an upright heart
    as I learn your righteous laws.
8 I will obey your decrees;
    do not utterly forsake me.

9 How can a young man keep his way pure?
    By living according to your word.
10 I seek you with all my heart;
    do not let me stray from your commands.
11 I have hidden your word in my heart
    that I might not sin against you.
12 Praise be to you, O Lord;
    teach me your decrees.
13 With my lips I recount
    all the laws that come from your mouth.
14 I rejoice in following your statutes
    as one rejoices in great riches.
15 I meditate on your precepts
    and consider your ways.
16 I delight in your decrees;
    I will not neglect your word.

17 Do good to your servant, and I will live;
    I will obey your word.
18 Open my eyes that I may see
    wonderful things in your law.
19 I am a stranger on earth;
    do not hide your commands from me.
20 My soul is consumed with longing
    for your laws at all times.

21 You rebuke the arrogant, who are cursed
    and who stray from your commands.
22 Remove from me scorn and contempt,
    for I keep your statutes.
23 Though rulers sit together and slander me,
    your servant will meditate on your decrees.
24 Your statutes are my delight;
    they are my counselors.

25 I am laid low in the dust;
    preserve my life according to your word.
26 I recounted my ways and you answered me;
    teach me your decrees.
27 Let me understand the teaching of your precepts;
    then I will meditate on your wonders.
28 My soul is weary with sorrow;
    strengthen me according to your word.
29 Keep me from deceitful ways;
    be gracious to me through your law.
30 I have chosen the way of truth;
    I have set my heart on your laws.
31 I hold fast to your statutes, O Lord;
    do not let me be put to shame.
32 I run in the path of your commands,
    for you have set my heart free.

33 Teach me, O Lord, to follow your decrees;
    then I will keep them to the end.
34 Give me understanding, and I will keep
        your law
    and obey it with all my heart.
35 Direct me in the path of your commands,
    for there I find delight.
36 Turn my heart toward your statutes
    and not toward selfish gain.

37 Turn my eyes away from worthless things;
   preserve my life according to your word. *ᵃ*

38 Fulfill your promise to your servant,
   so that you may be feared.

39 Take away the disgrace I dread,
   for your laws are good.

40 How I long for your precepts!
   Preserve my life in your righteousness.

41 May your unfailing love come to me, O Lord,
   your salvation according to your promise;

42 then I will answer the one who taunts me,
   for I trust in your word.

43 Do not snatch the word of truth from my mouth,
   for I have put my hope in your laws.

44 I will always obey your law,
   for ever and ever.

45 I will walk about in freedom,
   for I have sought out your precepts.

46 I will speak of your statutes before kings
   and will not be put to shame,

47 for I delight in your commands
   because I love them.

48 I lift up my hands to *ᵇ* your commands,
   which I love,
   and I meditate on your decrees.

49 Remember your word to your servant,
   for you have given me hope.

50 My comfort in my suffering is this:
   Your promise preserves my life.

ᵃ37 Two manuscripts of the Masoretic Text and Dead Sea Scrolls;
most manuscripts of the Masoretic Text *life in your way*   ᵇ48 Or *for*

51 The arrogant mock me without restraint,
     but I do not turn from your law.
52 I remember your ancient laws, O Lord,
     and I find comfort in them.
53 Indignation grips me because of the wicked,
     who have forsaken your law.
54 Your decrees are the theme of my song
     wherever I lodge.
55 In the night I remember your name, O Lord,
     and I will keep your law.
56 This has been my practice:
     I obey your precepts.

57 You are my portion, O Lord;
     I have promised to obey your words.
58 I have sought your face with all my heart;
     be gracious to me according to your promise.
59 I have considered my ways
     and have turned my steps to your statutes.
60 I will hasten and not delay
     to obey your commands.
61 Though the wicked bind me with ropes,
     I will not forget your law.
62 At midnight I rise to give you thanks
     for your righteous laws.
63 I am a friend to all who fear you,
     to all who follow your precepts.
64 The earth is filled with your love, O Lord;
     teach me your decrees.

65 Do good to your servant
     according to your word, O Lord.
66 Teach me knowledge and good judgment,
     for I believe in your commands.
67 Before I was afflicted I went astray,

but now I obey your word.
68 You are good, and what you do is good;
    teach me your decrees.
69 Though the arrogant have smeared me with lies,
    I keep your precepts with all my heart.
70 Their hearts are callous and unfeeling,
    but I delight in your law.
71 It was good for me to be afflicted
    so that I might learn your decrees.
72 The law from your mouth is more precious to me
    than thousands of pieces of silver and gold.

73 Your hands made me and formed me;
    give me understanding to learn your commands.
74 May those who fear you rejoice when they see
        me,
    for I have put my hope in your word.
75 I know, O Lord, that your laws are righteous,
    and in faithfulness you have afflicted me.
76 May your unfailing love be my comfort,
    according to your promise to your servant.
77 Let your compassion come to me that I may live,
    for your law is my delight.
78 May the arrogant be put to shame for wronging
        me without cause;
    but I will meditate on your precepts.
79 May those who fear you turn to me,
    those who understand your statutes.
80 May my heart be blameless toward your decrees,
    that I may not be put to shame.

81 My soul faints with longing for your salvation,
    but I have put my hope in your word.
82 My eyes fail, looking for your promise;
    I say, "When will you comfort me?"

83 Though I am like a wineskin in the smoke,
    I do not forget your decrees.
84 How long must your servant wait?
    When will you punish my persecutors?
85 The arrogant dig pitfalls for me,
    contrary to your law.
86 All your commands are trustworthy;
    help me, for men persecute me without cause.
87 They almost wiped me from the earth,
    but I have not forsaken your precepts.
88 Preserve my life according to your love,
    and I will obey the statutes of your mouth.

89 Your word, O Lord, is eternal;
    it stands firm in the heavens.
90 Your faithfulness continues through all
        generations;
    you established the earth, and it endures.
91 Your laws endure to this day,
    for all things serve you.
92 If your law had not been my delight,
    I would have perished in my affliction.
93 I will never forget your precepts,
    for by them you have preserved my life.
94 Save me, for I am yours;
    I have sought out your precepts.
95 The wicked are waiting to destroy me,
    but I will ponder your statutes.
96 To all perfection I see a limit;
    but your commands are boundless.

97 Oh, how I love your law!
    I meditate on it all day long.
98 Your commands make me wiser than my
        enemies,

for they are ever with me.
99 I have more insight than all my teachers,
   for I meditate on your statutes.
100 I have more understanding than the elders,
   for I obey your precepts.
101 I have kept my feet from every evil path
   so that I might obey your word.
102 I have not departed from your laws,
   for you yourself have taught me.
103 How sweet are your words to my taste,
   sweeter than honey to my mouth!
104 I gain understanding from your precepts;
   therefore I hate every wrong path.

105 Your word is a lamp to my feet
   and a light for my path.
106 I have taken an oath and confirmed it,
   that I will follow your righteous laws.
107 I have suffered much;
   preserve my life, O Lord, according to your word.
108 Accept, O Lord, the willing praise of my mouth,
   and teach me your laws.
109 Though I constantly take my life in my hands,
   I will not forget your law.
110 The wicked have set a snare for me,
   but I have not strayed from your precepts.
111 Your statutes are my heritage forever;
   they are the joy of my heart.
112 My heart is set on keeping your decrees
   to the very end.

113 I hate double-minded men,
   but I love your law.
114 You are my refuge and my shield;
   I have put my hope in your word.

115 Away from me, you evildoers,
   that I may keep the commands of my God!
116 Sustain me according to your promise,
      and I will live;
   do not let my hopes be dashed.
117 Uphold me, and I will be delivered;
   I will always have regard for your decrees.
118 You reject all who stray from your decrees,
   for their deceitfulness is in vain.
119 All the wicked of the earth you discard like
      dross;
   therefore I love your statutes.
120 My flesh trembles in fear of you;
   I stand in awe of your laws.

121 I have done what is righteous and just;
   do not leave me to my oppressors.
122 Ensure your servant's well-being;
   let not the arrogant oppress me.
123 My eyes fail, looking for your salvation,
   looking for your righteous promise.
124 Deal with your servant according to your love
   and teach me your decrees.
125 I am your servant; give me discernment
   that I may understand your statutes.
126 It is time for you to act, O Lord;
   your law is being broken.
127 Because I love your commands
   more than gold, more than pure gold,
128 and because I consider all your precepts
      right,
   I hate every wrong path.

129 Your statutes are wonderful;
   therefore I obey them.

130 The unfolding of your words gives light;
   it gives understanding to the simple.

131 I open my mouth and pant,
   longing for your commands.

132 Turn to me and have mercy on me,
   as you always do to those who love your
      name.

133 Direct my footsteps according to your word;
   let no sin rule over me.

134 Redeem me from the oppression of men,
   that I may obey your precepts.

135 Make your face shine upon your servant
   and teach me your decrees.

136 Streams of tears flow from my eyes,
   for your law is not obeyed.

137 Righteous are you, O Lord,
   and your laws are right.

138 The statutes you have laid down are righteous;
   they are fully trustworthy.

139 My zeal wears me out,
   for my enemies ignore your words.

140 Your promises have been thoroughly tested,
   and your servant loves them.

141 Though I am lowly and despised,
   I do not forget your precepts.

142 Your righteousness is everlasting
   and your law is true.

143 Trouble and distress have come upon me,
   but your commands are my delight.

144 Your statutes are forever right;
   give me understanding that I may live.

145 I call with all my heart; answer me, O Lord,
   and I will obey your decrees.

146 I call out to you; save me
and I will keep your statutes.
147 I rise before dawn and cry for help;
I have put my hope in your word.
148 My eyes stay open through the watches of the
night,
that I may meditate on your promises.
149 Hear my voice in accordance with your love;
preserve my life, O Lord, according to your
laws.
150 Those who devise wicked schemes are near,
but they are far from your law.
151 Yet you are near, O Lord,
and all your commands are true.
152 Long ago I learned from your statutes
that you established them to last forever.

153 Look upon my suffering and deliver me,
for I have not forgotten your law.
154 Defend my cause and redeem me;
preserve my life according to your promise.
155 Salvation is far from the wicked,
for they do not seek out your decrees.
156 Your compassion is great, O Lord;
preserve my life according to your laws.
157 Many are the foes who persecute me,
but I have not turned from your statutes.
158 I look on the faithless with loathing,
for they do not obey your word.
159 See how I love your precepts;
preserve my life, O Lord, according to your
love.
160 All your words are true;
all your righteous laws are eternal.

161 Rulers persecute me without cause,
　　but my heart trembles at your word.
162 I rejoice in your promise
　　like one who finds great spoil.
163 I hate and abhor falsehood
　　but I love your law.
164 Seven times a day I praise you
　　for your righteous laws.
165 Great peace have they who love your law,
　　and nothing can make them stumble.
166 I wait for your salvation, O Lord,
　　and I follow your commands.
167 I obey your statutes,
　　for I love them greatly.
168 I obey your precepts and your statutes,
　　for all my ways are known to you.

169 May my cry come before you, O Lord;
　　give me understanding according to your word.
170 May my supplication come before you;
　　deliver me according to your promise.
171 May my lips overflow with praise,
　　for you teach me your decrees.
172 May my tongue sing of your word,
　　for all your commands are righteous.
173 May your hand be ready to help me,
　　for I have chosen your precepts.
174 I long for your salvation, O Lord,
　　and your law is my delight.
175 Let me live that I may praise you,
　　and may your laws sustain me.
176 I have strayed like a lost sheep.
　　Seek your servant,
　　for I have not forgotten your commands.

Psalm 149

1 Praise the Lord. ^a

Sing to the Lord a new song,
  his praise in the assembly of the saints.

2 Let Israel rejoice in their Maker;
  let the people of Zion be glad in their King.
3 Let them praise his name with dancing
  and make music to him with tambourine and
    harp.
4 For the Lord takes delight in his people;
  he crowns the humble with salvation.
5 Let the saints rejoice in this honor
  and sing for joy on their beds.

6 May the praise of God be in their mouths
  and a double-edged sword in their hands,
7 to inflict vengeance on the nations
  and punishment on the peoples,
8 to bind their kings with fetters,
  their nobles with shackles of iron,
9 to carry out the sentence written against them.
  This is the glory of all his saints.

Praise the Lord.

Proverbs 29

1 A man who remains stiff-necked after many rebukes
  will suddenly be destroyed—without remedy.

2 When the righteous thrive, the people rejoice;
  when the wicked rule, the people groan.

---

^a1 Hebrew *Hallelu Yah;* also in verse 9

3 A man who loves wisdom brings joy to his father,
   but a companion of prostitutes squanders his
   wealth.

4 By justice a king gives a country stability,
   but one who is greedy for bribes tears it down.

5 Whoever flatters his neighbor
   is spreading a net for his feet.

6 An evil man is snared by his own sin,
   but a righteous one can sing and be glad.

7 The righteous care about justice for the poor,
   but the wicked have no such concern.

8 Mockers stir up a city,
   but wise men turn away anger.

9 If a wise man goes to court with a fool,
   the fool rages and scoffs, and there is no peace.

10 Bloodthirsty men hate a man of integrity
   and seek to kill the upright.

11 A fool gives full vent to his anger,
   but a wise man keeps himself under control.

12 If a ruler listens to lies,
   all his officials become wicked.

13 The poor man and the oppressor have this in
        common:
   The Lord gives sight to the eyes of both.

14 If a king judges the poor with fairness,
   his throne will always be secure.

15 The rod of correction imparts wisdom,
   but a child left to himself disgraces his mother.

16 When the wicked thrive, so does sin,
     but the righteous will see their downfall.

17 Discipline your son, and he will give you peace;
     he will bring delight to your soul.

18 Where there is no revelation, the people cast off
           restraint;
     but blessed is he who keeps the law.

19 A servant cannot be corrected by mere words;
     though he understands, he will not respond.

20 Do you see a man who speaks in haste?
     There is more hope for a fool than for him.

21 If a man pampers his servant from youth,
     he will bring grief *a* in the end.

22 An angry man stirs up dissension,
     and a hot-tempered one commits many sins.

23 A man's pride brings him low,
     but a man of lowly spirit gains honor.

24 The accomplice of a thief is his own enemy;
     he is put under oath and dare not testify.

25 Fear of man will prove to be a snare,
     but whoever trusts in the Lord is kept safe.

26 Many seek an audience with a ruler,
     but it is from the Lord that man gets justice.

27 The righteous detest the dishonest;
     the wicked detest the upright.

*a*21 The meaning of the Hebrew for this word is uncertain.

DAY 30

Psalm 30

A psalm. A song. For the dedication of the temple. [a]
Of David.

1   I will exalt you, O Lord,
        for you lifted me out of the depths
        and did not let my enemies gloat over me.

2   O Lord my God, I called to you for help
        and you healed me.

3   O Lord, you brought me up from the grave [b];
        you spared me from going down into the pit.

4   Sing to the Lord, you saints of his;
        praise his holy name.

5   For his anger lasts only a moment,
        but his favor lasts a lifetime;
    weeping may remain for a night,
        but rejoicing comes in the morning.

6   When I felt secure, I said,
        "I will never be shaken."

7   O Lord, when you favored me,
        you made my mountain [c] stand firm;
    but when you hid your face,
        I was dismayed.

8   To you, O Lord, I called;
        to the Lord I cried for mercy:

9   "What gain is there in my destruction, [d]
        in my going down into the pit?

---

[a] Title: Or *palace*   [b]3 Hebrew *Sheol*   [c]7 Or *hill country*   [d]9 Or
there if I am silenced

Will the dust praise you?
    Will it proclaim your faithfulness?
10 Hear, O Lord, and be merciful to me;
    O Lord, be my help."

11 You turned my wailing into dancing;
    you removed my sackcloth and clothed me
        with joy,
12 that my heart may sing to you and not be silent.
    O Lord my God, I will give you thanks forever.

Psalm 60

For the director of music. To the tune of "The Lily of
the Covenant." A *miktam* ^a of David. For teaching.
When he fought Aram Naharaim ^b and Aram
Zobah, ^c and when Joab returned and struck down
twelve thousand Edomites in the Valley of Salt.

1   You have rejected us, O God, and burst
        forth upon us;
    you have been angry—now restore us!
2   You have shaken the land and torn it open;
    mend its fractures, for it is quaking.
3   You have shown your people desperate times;
    you have given us wine that makes us
        stagger.
4   But for those who fear you, you have raised a
        banner
    to be unfurled against the bow.   *Selah*

^a Title: Probably a literary or musical term   ^b Title: That is,
Arameans of Northwest Mesopotamia   ^c Title: That is, Arameans
of central Syria

5 Save us and help us with your right hand,
  that those you love may be delivered.
6 God has spoken from his sanctuary:
  "In triumph I will parcel out Shechem
  and measure off the Valley of Succoth.
7 Gilead is mine, and Manasseh is mine;
  Ephraim is my helmet,
  Judah my scepter.
8 Moab is my washbasin,
  upon Edom I toss my sandal;
  over Philistia I shout in triumph."

9 Who will bring me to the fortified city?
  Who will lead me to Edom?
10 Is it not you, O God, you who have rejected
   us
   and no longer go out with our armies?
11 Give us aid against the enemy,
   for the help of man is worthless.
12 With God we will gain the victory,
   and he will trample down our enemies.

Psalm 90
A prayer of Moses the man of God.

1 Lord, you have been our dwelling place
  throughout all generations.
2 Before the mountains were born
  or you brought forth the earth and
  the world,
  from everlasting to everlasting you
  are God.

3 You turn men back to dust,
  saying, "Return to dust, O sons of men."

4   For a thousand years in your sight
        are like a day that has just gone by,
        or like a watch in the night.
5   You sweep men away in the sleep of death;
        they are like the new grass of the morning—
6   though in the morning it springs up new,
        by evening it is dry and withered.

7   We are consumed by your anger
        and terrified by your indignation.
8   You have set our iniquities before you,
        our secret sins in the light of your presence.
9   All our days pass away under your wrath;
        we finish our years with a moan.
10 The length of our days is seventy years—
        or eighty, if we have the strength;
        yet their span *a* is but trouble and sorrow,
        for they quickly pass, and we fly away.

11 Who knows the power of your anger?
        For your wrath is as great as the fear that
            is due you.
12 Teach us to number our days aright,
        that we may gain a heart of wisdom.

13 Relent, O Lord! How long will it be?
        Have compassion on your servants.
14 Satisfy us in the morning with your unfailing
            love,
        that we may sing for joy and be glad all our
            days.
15 Make us glad for as many days as you have
            afflicted us,

a10 Or *yet the best of them*

for as many years as we have seen trouble.
16 May your deeds be shown to your servants,
your splendor to their children.

17 May the favor [a] of the Lord our God rest
upon us;
establish the work of our hands for us—
yes, establish the work of our hands.

Psalm 120
A song of ascents.

1 I call on the Lord in my distress,
and he answers me.
2 Save me, O Lord, from lying lips
and from deceitful tongues.

3 What will he do to you,
and what more besides, O deceitful
tongue?
4 He will punish you with a warrior's
sharp arrows,
with burning coals of the broom tree.

5 Woe to me that I dwell in Meshech,
that I live among the tents of Kedar!
6 Too long have I lived
among those who hate peace.
7 I am a man of peace;
but when I speak, they are for war.

[a] 17 Or beauty

Psalm 150

1   Praise the Lord. [a]

Praise God in his sanctuary;
    praise him in his mighty heavens.
2   Praise him for his acts of power;
    praise him for his surpassing greatness.
3   Praise him with the sounding of the trumpet,
    praise him with the harp and lyre,
4   praise him with tambourine and dancing,
    praise him with the strings and flute,
5   praise him with the clash of cymbals,
    praise him with resounding cymbals.

6   Let everything that has breath praise the Lord.

Praise the Lord.

Proverbs 30

1   The sayings of Agur son of Jakeh—an oracle [b]:

This man declared to Ithiel,
    to Ithiel and to Ucal: [c]

2   "I am the most ignorant of men;
    I do not have a man's understanding.
3   I have not learned wisdom,
    nor have I knowledge of the Holy One.
4   Who has gone up to heaven and come down?

---

[a]1 Hebrew *Hallelu Yah;* also in verse 6   [b]1 Or *Jakeh of Massa*
[c]1 Masoretic Text; with a different word division of the Hebrew
declared, "I am weary, O God; / I am weary, O God, and faint.

Who has gathered up the wind in the hollow of
    his hands?
Who has wrapped up the waters in his cloak?
    Who has established all the ends of the earth?
What is his name, and the name of his son?
    Tell me if you know!

5 "Every word of God is flawless;
    he is a shield to those who take refuge in him.
6 Do not add to his words,
    or he will rebuke you and prove you a liar.

7 "Two things I ask of you, O Lord;
    do not refuse me before I die:
8 Keep falsehood and lies far from me;
    give me neither poverty nor riches,
    but give me only my daily bread.
9 Otherwise, I may have too much and disown
      you
    and say, 'Who is the Lord?'
  Or I may become poor and steal,
    and so dishonor the name of my God.

10 "Do not slander a servant to his master,
    or he will curse you, and you will pay for it.

11 "There are those who curse their fathers
    and do not bless their mothers;
12 those who are pure in their own eyes
    and yet are not cleansed of their filth;
13 those whose eyes are ever so haughty,
    whose glances are so disdainful;
14 those whose teeth are swords
    and whose jaws are set with knives
to devour the poor from the earth,
    the needy from among mankind.

15 "The leech has two daughters.
    'Give! Give!' they cry.

"There are three things that are never satisfied,
    four that never say, 'Enough!':
16 the grave, ^a the barren womb,
    land, which is never satisfied with water,
    and fire, which never says, 'Enough!'

17 "The eye that mocks a father,
    that scorns obedience to a mother,
will be pecked out by the ravens of the valley,
    will be eaten by the vultures.

18 "There are three things that are too amazing
        for me,
    four that I do not understand:
19 the way of an eagle in the sky,
    the way of a snake on a rock,
the way of a ship on the high seas,
    and the way of a man with a maiden.

20 "This is the way of an adulteress:
    She eats and wipes her mouth
    and says, 'I've done nothing wrong.'

21 "Under three things the earth trembles,
    under four it cannot bear up:
22 a servant who becomes king,
    a fool who is full of food,
23 an unloved woman who is married,
    and a maidservant who displaces her
        mistress.

^a16 Hebrew *Sheol*

24 "Four things on earth are small,
    yet they are extremely wise:
25 Ants are creatures of little strength,
    yet they store up their food in the summer;
26 coneys [a] are creatures of little power,
    yet they make their home in the crags;
27 locusts have no king,
    yet they advance together in ranks;
28 a lizard can be caught with the hand,
    yet it is found in kings' palaces.

29 "There are three things that are stately in their
       stride,
    four that move with stately bearing:
30 a lion, mighty among beasts,
    who retreats before nothing;
31 a strutting rooster, a he-goat,
    and a king with his army around him. [b]

32 "If you have played the fool and exalted
       yourself,
    or if you have planned evil,
    clap your hand over your mouth!
33 For as churning the milk produces butter,
    and as twisting the nose produces blood,
    so stirring up anger produces strife."

[a]26 That is, the hyrax or rock badger   [b]31 Or king secure against
revolt

DAY 31

Psalm 31
For the director of music. A psalm of David.

1 In you, O Lord, I have taken refuge;
    let me never be put to shame;
    deliver me in your righteousness.
2 Turn your ear to me,
    come quickly to my rescue;
    be my rock of refuge,
    a strong fortress to save me.
3 Since you are my rock and my fortress,
    for the sake of your name lead and guide me.
4 Free me from the trap that is set for me,
    for you are my refuge.
5 Into your hands I commit my spirit;
    redeem me, O Lord, the God of truth.
6 I hate those who cling to worthless idols;
    I trust in the Lord.
7 I will be glad and rejoice in your love,
    for you saw my affliction
    and knew the anguish of my soul.
8 You have not handed me over to the enemy
    but have set my feet in a spacious place.

9 Be merciful to me, O Lord, for I am in distress;
    my eyes grow weak with sorrow,
    my soul and my body with grief.
10 My life is consumed by anguish
    and my years by groaning;
    my strength fails because of my affliction, *a*

a10 Or *guilt*

and my bones grow weak.
11 Because of all my enemies,
    I am the utter contempt of my neighbors;
I am a dread to my friends—
    those who see me on the street flee from me.
12 I am forgotten by them as though I were dead;
    I have become like broken pottery.
13 For I hear the slander of many;
    there is terror on every side;
they conspire against me
    and plot to take my life.

14 But I trust in you, O Lord;
    I say, "You are my God."
15 My times are in your hands;
    deliver me from my enemies
    and from those who pursue me.
16 Let your face shine on your servant;
    save me in your unfailing love.
17 Let me not be put to shame, O Lord,
    for I have cried out to you;
but let the wicked be put to shame
    and lie silent in the grave. *a*
18 Let their lying lips be silenced,
    for with pride and contempt
    they speak arrogantly against the righteous.

19 How great is your goodness,
    which you have stored up for those who fear
        you,
which you bestow in the sight of men
    on those who take refuge in you.

*a*17 Hebrew *Sheol*

20 In the shelter of your presence you hide them
        from the intrigues of men;
    in your dwelling you keep them safe
        from accusing tongues.

21 Praise be to the Lord,
        for he showed his wonderful love to me
        when I was in a besieged city.
22 In my alarm I said,
        "I am cut off from your sight!"
    Yet you heard my cry for mercy
        when I called to you for help.

23 Love the Lord, all his saints!
        The Lord preserves the faithful,
        but the proud he pays back in full.
24 Be strong and take heart,
        all you who hope in the Lord.

Psalm 119 *a*

1   Blessed are they whose ways are blameless,
        who walk according to the law of the Lord.
2   Blessed are they who keep his statutes
        and seek him with all their heart.
3   They do nothing wrong;
        they walk in his ways.
4   You have laid down precepts
        that are to be fully obeyed.
5   Oh, that my ways were steadfast
        in obeying your decrees!

---

a This psalm is an acrostic poem; the verses of each stanza begin with
the same letter of the Hebrew alphabet.

6 Then I would not be put to shame
   when I consider all your commands.
7 I will praise you with an upright heart
   as I learn your righteous laws.
8 I will obey your decrees;
   do not utterly forsake me.

9 How can a young man keep his way pure?
   By living according to your word.
10 I seek you with all my heart;
   do not let me stray from your commands.
11 I have hidden your word in my heart
   that I might not sin against you.
12 Praise be to you, O Lord;
   teach me your decrees.
13 With my lips I recount
   all the laws that come from your mouth.
14 I rejoice in following your statutes
   as one rejoices in great riches.
15 I meditate on your precepts
   and consider your ways.
16 I delight in your decrees;
   I will not neglect your word.

17 Do good to your servant, and I will live;
   I will obey your word.
18 Open my eyes that I may see
   wonderful things in your law.
19 I am a stranger on earth;
   do not hide your commands from me.
20 My soul is consumed with longing
   for your laws at all times.
21 You rebuke the arrogant, who are cursed
   and who stray from your commands.

22 Remove from me scorn and contempt,
   for I keep your statutes.
23 Though rulers sit together and slander me,
   your servant will meditate on your decrees.
24 Your statutes are my delight;
   they are my counselors.

25 I am laid low in the dust;
   preserve my life according to your word.
26 I recounted my ways and you answered me;
   teach me your decrees.
27 Let me understand the teaching of your
      precepts;
   then I will meditate on your wonders.
28 My soul is weary with sorrow;
   strengthen me according to your word.
29 Keep me from deceitful ways;
   be gracious to me through your law.
30 I have chosen the way of truth;
   I have set my heart on your laws.
31 I hold fast to your statutes, O Lord;
   do not let me be put to shame.
32 I run in the path of your commands,
   for you have set my heart free.

33 Teach me, O Lord, to follow your decrees;
   then I will keep them to the end.
34 Give me understanding, and I will keep
      your law
   and obey it with all my heart.
35 Direct me in the path of your commands,
   for there I find delight.
36 Turn my heart toward your statutes
   and not toward selfish gain.

37 Turn my eyes away from worthless things;
    preserve my life according to your word. [a]

38 Fulfill your promise to your servant,
    so that you may be feared.

39 Take away the disgrace I dread,
    for your laws are good.

40 How I long for your precepts!
    Preserve my life in your righteousness.

41 May your unfailing love come to me, O Lord,
    your salvation according to your promise;

42 then I will answer the one who taunts me,
    for I trust in your word.

43 Do not snatch the word of truth from my mouth,
    for I have put my hope in your laws.

44 I will always obey your law,
    for ever and ever.

45 I will walk about in freedom,
    for I have sought out your precepts.

46 I will speak of your statutes before kings
    and will not be put to shame,

47 for I delight in your commands
    because I love them.

48 I lift up my hands to [b] your commands,
        which I love,
    and I meditate on your decrees.

49 Remember your word to your servant,
    for you have given me hope.

50 My comfort in my suffering is this:
    Your promise preserves my life.

---

[a]37 Two manuscripts of the Masoretic Text and Dead Sea Scrolls;
most manuscripts of the Masoretic Text *life in your way*   [b]48 Or *for*

51 The arrogant mock me without restraint,
   but I do not turn from your law.
52 I remember your ancient laws, O Lord,
   and I find comfort in them.
53 Indignation grips me because of the wicked,
   who have forsaken your law.
54 Your decrees are the theme of my song
   wherever I lodge.
55 In the night I remember your name, O Lord,
   and I will keep your law.
56 This has been my practice:
   I obey your precepts.

57 You are my portion, O Lord;
   I have promised to obey your words.
58 I have sought your face with all my heart;
   be gracious to me according to your promise.
59 I have considered my ways
   and have turned my steps to your statutes.
60 I will hasten and not delay
   to obey your commands.
61 Though the wicked bind me with ropes,
   I will not forget your law.
62 At midnight I rise to give you thanks
   for your righteous laws.
63 I am a friend to all who fear you,
   to all who follow your precepts.
64 The earth is filled with your love, O Lord;
   teach me your decrees.

65 Do good to your servant
   according to your word, O Lord.
66 Teach me knowledge and good judgment,
   for I believe in your commands.
67 Before I was afflicted I went astray,

but now I obey your word.
68 You are good, and what you do is good;
teach me your decrees.
69 Though the arrogant have smeared me with
lies,
I keep your precepts with all my heart.
70 Their hearts are callous and unfeeling,
but I delight in your law.
71 It was good for me to be afflicted
so that I might learn your decrees.
72 The law from your mouth is more precious to
me
than thousands of pieces of silver and gold.

73 Your hands made me and formed me;
give me understanding to learn your commands.
74 May those who fear you rejoice when they see
me,
for I have put my hope in your word.
75 I know, O Lord, that your laws are righteous,
and in faithfulness you have afflicted me.
76 May your unfailing love be my comfort,
according to your promise to your servant.
77 Let your compassion come to me that I may
live,
for your law is my delight.
78 May the arrogant be put to shame for wronging
me without cause;
but I will meditate on your precepts.
79 May those who fear you turn to me,
those who understand your statutes.
80 May my heart be blameless toward your
decrees,
that I may not be put to shame.

81 My soul faints with longing for your salvation,
    but I have put my hope in your word.

82 My eyes fail, looking for your promise;
    I say, "When will you comfort me?"

83 Though I am like a wineskin in the smoke,
    I do not forget your decrees.

84 How long must your servant wait?
    When will you punish my persecutors?

85 The arrogant dig pitfalls for me,
    contrary to your law.

86 All your commands are trustworthy;
    help me, for men persecute me without cause.

87 They almost wiped me from the earth,
    but I have not forsaken your precepts.

88 Preserve my life according to your love,
    and I will obey the statutes of your mouth.

89 Your word, O Lord, is eternal;
    it stands firm in the heavens.

90 Your faithfulness continues through all
      generations;
    you established the earth, and it endures.

91 Your laws endure to this day,
    for all things serve you.

92 If your law had not been my delight,
    I would have perished in my affliction.

93 I will never forget your precepts,
    for by them you have preserved my life.

94 Save me, for I am yours;
    I have sought out your precepts.

95 The wicked are waiting to destroy me,
    but I will ponder your statutes.

96 To all perfection I see a limit;
    but your commands are boundless.

97 Oh, how I love your law!
       I meditate on it all day long.
98 Your commands make me wiser than my
         enemies,
       for they are ever with me.
99 I have more insight than all my teachers,
       for I meditate on your statutes.
100 I have more understanding than the elders,
       for I obey your precepts.
101 I have kept my feet from every evil path
       so that I might obey your word.
102 I have not departed from your laws,
       for you yourself have taught me.
103 How sweet are your words to my taste,
       sweeter than honey to my mouth!
104 I gain understanding from your precepts;
       therefore I hate every wrong path.

105 Your word is a lamp to my feet
       and a light for my path.
106 I have taken an oath and confirmed it,
       that I will follow your righteous laws.
107 I have suffered much;
       preserve my life, O Lord, according to
          your word.
108 Accept, O Lord, the willing praise of my mouth,
       and teach me your laws.
109 Though I constantly take my life in my hands,
       I will not forget your law.
110 The wicked have set a snare for me,
       but I have not strayed from your precepts.
111 Your statutes are my heritage forever;
       they are the joy of my heart.

112 My heart is set on keeping your decrees
      to the very end.

113 I hate double-minded men,
      but I love your law.

114 You are my refuge and my shield;
      I have put my hope in your word.

115 Away from me, you evildoers,
      that I may keep the commands of my God!

116 Sustain me according to your promise,
      and I will live;
      do not let my hopes be dashed.

117 Uphold me, and I will be delivered;
      I will always have regard for your decrees.

118 You reject all who stray from your decrees,
      for their deceitfulness is in vain.

119 All the wicked of the earth you discard like
      dross;
      therefore I love your statutes.

120 My flesh trembles in fear of you;
      I stand in awe of your laws.

121 I have done what is righteous and just;
      do not leave me to my oppressors.

122 Ensure your servant's well-being;
      let not the arrogant oppress me.

123 My eyes fail, looking for your salvation,
      looking for your righteous promise.

124 Deal with your servant according to your love
      and teach me your decrees.

125 I am your servant; give me discernment
      that I may understand your statutes.

126 It is time for you to act, O Lord;
      your law is being broken.

127 Because I love your commands
  more than gold, more than pure gold,
128 and because I consider all your precepts right,
  I hate every wrong path.

129 Your statutes are wonderful;
  therefore I obey them.
130 The unfolding of your words gives light;
  it gives understanding to the simple.
131 I open my mouth and pant,
  longing for your commands.
132 Turn to me and have mercy on me,
  as you always do to those who love your
    name.
133 Direct my footsteps according to your word;
  let no sin rule over me.
134 Redeem me from the oppression of men,
  that I may obey your precepts.
135 Make your face shine upon your servant
  and teach me your decrees.
136 Streams of tears flow from my eyes,
  for your law is not obeyed.

137 Righteous are you, O Lord,
  and your laws are right.
138 The statutes you have laid down are righteous;
  they are fully trustworthy.
139 My zeal wears me out,
  for my enemies ignore your words.
140 Your promises have been thoroughly tested,
  and your servant loves them.
141 Though I am lowly and despised,
  I do not forget your precepts.
142 Your righteousness is everlasting
  and your law is true.

¹⁴³ Trouble and distress have come upon me,
   but your commands are my delight.
¹⁴⁴ Your statutes are forever right;
   give me understanding that I may live.

¹⁴⁵ I call with all my heart; answer me, O Lord,
   and I will obey your decrees.
¹⁴⁶ I call out to you; save me
   and I will keep your statutes.
¹⁴⁷ I rise before dawn and cry for help;
   I have put my hope in your word.
¹⁴⁸ My eyes stay open through the watches of the
      night,
   that I may meditate on your promises.
¹⁴⁹ Hear my voice in accordance with your love;
   preserve my life, O Lord, according to your
      laws.
¹⁵⁰ Those who devise wicked schemes are near,
   but they are far from your law.
¹⁵¹ Yet you are near, O Lord,
   and all your commands are true.
¹⁵² Long ago I learned from your statutes
   that you established them to last forever.

¹⁵³ Look upon my suffering and deliver me,
   for I have not forgotten your law.
¹⁵⁴ Defend my cause and redeem me;
   preserve my life according to your promise.
¹⁵⁵ Salvation is far from the wicked,
   for they do not seek out your decrees.
¹⁵⁶ Your compassion is great, O Lord;
   preserve my life according to your laws.
¹⁵⁷ Many are the foes who persecute me,
   but I have not turned from your statutes.

158 I look on the faithless with loathing,
　　　for they do not obey your word.
159 See how I love your precepts;
　　　preserve my life, O Lord, according to your
　　　　　love.
160 All your words are true;
　　　all your righteous laws are eternal.

161 Rulers persecute me without cause,
　　　but my heart trembles at your word.
162 I rejoice in your promise
　　　like one who finds great spoil.
163 I hate and abhor falsehood
　　　but I love your law.
164 Seven times a day I praise you
　　　for your righteous laws.
165 Great peace have they who love your law,
　　　and nothing can make them stumble.
166 I wait for your salvation, O Lord,
　　　and I follow your commands.
167 I obey your statutes,
　　　for I love them greatly.
168 I obey your precepts and your statutes,
　　　for all my ways are known to you.

169 May my cry come before you, O Lord;
　　　give me understanding according to
　　　　　your word.
170 May my supplication come before you;
　　　deliver me according to your promise.
171 May my lips overflow with praise,
　　　for you teach me your decrees.
172 May my tongue sing of your word,
　　　for all your commands are righteous.

173 May your hand be ready to help me,
    for I have chosen your precepts.
174 I long for your salvation, O Lord,
    and your law is my delight.
175 Let me live that I may praise you,
    and may your laws sustain me.
176 I have strayed like a lost sheep.
    Seek your servant,
    for I have not forgotten your commands.

Proverbs 31

1 The sayings of King Lemuel—an oracle *a* his mother taught him:

2 "O my son, O son of my womb,
    O son of my vows, *b*
3 do not spend your strength on women,
    your vigor on those who ruin kings.

4 "It is not for kings, O Lemuel—
    not for kings to drink wine,
    not for rulers to crave beer,
5 lest they drink and forget what the law decrees,
    and deprive all the oppressed of their rights.
6 Give beer to those who are perishing,
    wine to those who are in anguish;
7 let them drink and forget their poverty
    and remember their misery no more.

8 "Speak up for those who cannot speak for
    themselves,
    for the rights of all who are destitute.

*a*1 Or *of Lemuel king of Massa, which*   *b*2 Or / *the answer to my prayers*

9 Speak up and judge fairly;
    defend the rights of the poor and needy."

10 ^a A wife of noble character who can find?
    She is worth far more than rubies.
11 Her husband has full confidence in her
    and lacks nothing of value.
12 She brings him good, not harm,
    all the days of her life.
13 She selects wool and flax
    and works with eager hands.
14 She is like the merchant ships,
    bringing her food from afar.
15 She gets up while it is still dark;
    she provides food for her family
    and portions for her servant girls.
16 She considers a field and buys it;
    out of her earnings she plants a vineyard.
17 She sets about her work vigorously;
    her arms are strong for her tasks.
18 She sees that her trading is profitable,
    and her lamp does not go out at night.
19 In her hand she holds the distaff
    and grasps the spindle with her fingers.
20 She opens her arms to the poor
    and extends her hands to the needy.
21 When it snows, she has no fear for her household;
    for all of them are clothed in scarlet.
22 She makes coverings for her bed;
    she is clothed in fine linen and purple.
23 Her husband is respected at the city gate,

---

^a10 Verses 10-31 are an acrostic, each verse beginning with a
successive letter of the Hebrew alphabet.

where he takes his seat among the elders of the
land.

24 She makes linen garments and sells them,
and supplies the merchants with sashes.

25 She is clothed with strength and dignity;
she can laugh at the days to come.

26 She speaks with wisdom,
and faithful instruction is on her tongue.

27 She watches over the affairs of her household
and does not eat the bread of idleness.

28 Her children arise and call her blessed;
her husband also, and he praises her:

29 "Many women do noble things,
but you surpass them all."

30 Charm is deceptive, and beauty is fleeting;
but a woman who fears the Lord is to be
praised.

31 Give her the reward she has earned,
and let her works bring her praise at the city
gate.

INDEX TO PSALMS AND PROVERBS

Day	Psalm					Proverbs
16	16	46	76	106	136	16
17	17	47	77	107	137	17
18	18	48	78	108	138	18
19	19	49	79	109	139	19
20	20	50	80	110	140	20
21	21	51	81	111	141	21
22	22	52	82	112	142	22
23	23	53	83	113	143	23
24	24	54	84	114	144	24
25	25	55	85	115	145	25
26	26	56	86	116	146	26
27	27	57	87	117	147	27
28	28	58	88	118	148	28
29	29	59	89	119	149	29
30	30	60	90	120	150	30
31	31	119				31